W9-COJ-033

The Choice of Pension Plans in a Changing Regulatory Environment

The Choice of Pension Plans in a Changing Regulatory Environment

Robert L. Clark and
Ann A. McDermed

The AEI Press

Publisher for the American Enterprise Institute
WASHINGTON, D. C.

1990

331.252
C 594

Library of Congress Cataloging-in-Publication Data

Clark, Robert Louis, 1949–
  The choice of pension plans in a changing regulatory environment /
Robert Clark & Ann McDermed.
    p. cm.
  Includes bibliographical references (p.
  ISBN 0-8447-3725-9 (alk. paper).
    1. Pension trusts—United States.   2. Compensation management—
United States.   I. McDermed, Ann Archibald, 1941–   .   II. Title.
HD7105.45.U6C53   1990
658.3'253—dc20   90-213
                                                                    CIP

AEI Studies 509

Printed in the United States of America

Contents

Acknowledgments

Our initial research examining the trends toward greater use of defined contribution plans was supported by a grant from the Office of Pension and Welfare Benefit Programs, U.S. Department of Labor. Gary Hendricks and Daniel Beller of that office have been most helpful in our study of the 5500 data. Carolyn Weaver, Richard Ippolito, and several anonymous referees have provided numerous useful comments on earlier drafts of this manuscript. Some of our findings are based on previous research in which Steven Allen was an important collaborator. Stephen Gohmann assisted us with our initial evaluation of the 5500 data.

1
Pensions and Regulation

Since the mid-1970s, the private pension system in the United States has undergone considerable change. The most notable development has been the increasing reliance on defined contribution plans over the traditional defined benefit plans. Between 1980 and 1985 alone, the number of primary defined contribution plans increased by 71 percent and the number of participants rose by 83 percent; in contrast, primary defined benefit coverage showed virtually no growth (table 1–1). Although both types of pensions provide retirement income, they differ greatly in their effect on worker behavior and the risks that are borne by workers and firms with respect to the value of future benefits.

The principal objective of this study is to assess the extent of the change in pension coverage by plan type since 1974, and to explain the observed shift toward defined contribution plans. This shift has occurred under the pressure of increasing federal pension regulation since the passage of the Employee Retirement Income Security Act (ERISA) in 1974 and appears to reflect a change in the pension choice process. The effects of federal policy have been bolstered by structural changes in the American economy and a decline in unionization, which have shifted the employment base toward jobs traditionally covered by defined contribution plans.

In mandating greater pension security to covered workers, ERISA and subsequent legislation have reduced the incentive of workers and employers to seek defined benefit plans. In the past, these plans were a means of raising productivity, reducing costs, and increasing employee compensation. Government regulations that discourage the use of these plans jeopardize the efficiency of employment contracts and may produce an adverse effect on the economy.

Pensions and Employee Compensation

Pensions are a form of deferred compensation that many firms offer their workers. In essence, workers exchange a portion of their current labor for the promise of future payment in retirement. Workers are

TABLE 1-1

NUMBER OF PRIMARY PENSION PLANS AND PARTICIPANTS
BY PLAN TYPE, 1980 AND 1985

Plan Type	Plans		Participants (millions)	
	1980	1985	1980	1985
Defined benefit	22,010	23,174	26.4	26.7
	(74.7)	(64.7)	(87.1)	(78.7)
Defined contribution	7,271	12,427	3.6	6.9
	(24.7)	(34.7)	(11.9)	(20.4)

NOTE: These data are limited to primary plans of 100 or more participants. The numbers in parentheses represent the percentage of all plans or participants covered by the indicated plan type. The percentage do not add to 100 because they include a small number of other plan types.
SOURCE: 5500 Tax Reporting Forms, 1980 and 1985.

willing to make such an exchange if it increases their lifetime income and if they believe that their employers will honor the pension promise (or the promise is explictly stated in a legal contract).

In the absence of government regulation, firms and workers could engage in negotiations concerning the amount of labor compensation to be allocated during each pay period to current earnings and to funding future pension benefits. The two parties could then determine the structure of the pension plan that best meets their joint objectives. Theoretically, pensions could be tailored to individual workers. Owing to administrative costs, however, pensions have generally been designed for groups of workers who have similar levels of income, tax rates, and preferences concerning the lifetime pattern of consumption and savings and the amount of risk they are willing to take.[1]

Employer-sponsored pension plans in the United States consist of two basic types: defined contribution and defined benefit plans. Historically, defined benefit plans were more likely to be found in large unionized firms, and defined contribution plans in smaller, nonunion firms. The two plans differ, first, in the method used to determine retirement benefits. In defined contribution plans, employers promise to transfer a specified amount of money each period into each worker's pension account. The retirement benefit is determined by the value of the fund when the worker leaves the firm. Defined benefit plans, by contrast, promise each worker a specified benefit, and the firm is obliged to pay it. Each type of plan stipulates the

2

method used to calculate the value of the pension to the worker and the cost to the firm.

Second, the plans differ in the financial and labor market risks borne by workers and firms. Pension-related risks are those surrounding the rate of return on pension funds, the rate of inflation while working, and the rate of inflation after retirement, and job security risks (such as the termination of employment, job changes, or firm failure). The level and type of risk is a prime factor in the decision of firms and workers to choose one type of plan over another. Even without any government regulation or tax inducements, some workers and firms would select defined benefit plans, whereas others would favor defined contribution plans. The choice would depend on which plan is expected to maximize income in the case of the worker, and profits, in the case of the firm. In the relatively unregulated environment before 1974, most workers and firms clearly preferred defined benefit plans. Since then, defined contribution plans have gained considerable ground, as we document in the following chapters through a careful examination of the tax forms that plan sponsors are required to file with the Internal Revenue Service each year.

Pensions and Efficient Employment Contracts

Defined benefit plans offer workers a specified pension conditional on their fulfilling the terms of an implicit employment contract. One of the terms of such contracts is that workers must remain with the firm until retirement and perform at an agreed-upon level if they wish to qualify for the full retirement annuity defined by the pension formula. Those who leave the firm before retirement are usually penalized a specified amount. This pension penalty tends to tie the worker to the firm and thus to reduce turnover. Lower turnover reduces the firm's labor costs and allows it to invest more in the worker. Lower labor costs and higher productivity enable the firm to pay its workers higher lifetime compensation in conjunction with the pension contract. Firms try to entice workers to accept these contracts by offering them a lifetime wage profile and by reducing the chances of layoff.

Defined benefit plans may also be used to provide older workers with large economic incentives to retire. They may stipulate, for example, that the total gain from working will drop sharply at a certain age. Thus, firms can use these plans to achieve the desired age structure of their labor force.

In contrast, the defined contribution plan cannot be used to tie workers to a firm or to give them added incentives to retire. The incentives provided by this type of plan can be compared to cash earnings. The employer may encourage the worker to remain with the firm by offering more overall compensation, including higher contributions to the pension, but firms cannot impose a pension penalty on workers who quit their jobs. The defined benefit plan is more likely to be adopted in firms that stand to make the greatest gains from employment contracts that reduce mobility. Where such contracts are in effect, productivity increases and consequently firms are able to increase the lifetime income of workers who complete the terms of the contract. Workers who violate the contract by quitting or who are laid off because they performed at substandard levels lose lifetime wealth.

After entering into pension contracts, firms have a short-run incentive to violate the contract by firing older workers. The firm could reap the advantage of the workers' relatively long worklife and then fire them before they accumulate the maximum possible pension. The firm, however, has a labor market reputation to consider and no doubt wants to continue making employment contracts with younger workers, so that it is not in the firm's long-run interest to violate the contract. If a firm tells new employees that it has a no-layoff policy and then systematically fires older workers, for example, new applicants are not likely to believe the no-layoff promise and thus will not be willing to incur the wage concessions sought by firms to fund the pension promise.

Concerns about the Pension Contract

The pension contract can run into problems if there is a long lag between the time that pension credits are earned and the time that benefits are paid. This time interval creates uncertainty as to whether workers will eventually receive any pension benefits. If they have a way of assessing the risks associated with these contracts, however, they can determine the expected value of the pension promise, and the wages they are willing to forgo to get that promise. To make such an assessment, they must have access to a great deal of information— on employer pension contributions, the administration of the pension fund, investment performance of the fund, and the future of the firm. In addition, workers must know how to use the data to calculate whether enough pension funds will be available in twenty or thirty years to pay for their benefits.

The fact that defined benefit pensions accrue over a long period and are often based on complex formulas makes it difficult to determine their true value. One reason for government intervention has been to ensure that workers receive adequate information about their pensions. The government has also mandated funding standards in order to discourage firms from defaulting on their pension promises.

In principle, funding standards and reporting requirements do not conflict with the basic objective of defined benefit plans as they relate to the employment contract. In practice, they have increased the cost of operating defined benefit plans in comparison with defined contribution plans.

Regulations that seek to reduce or eliminate the pension penalty for leaving the firm strike at the heart of the pension contract. Reduced vesting and participation standards along with portable pension credits tend to promote mobility by lowering the cost of changing jobs. Such initiatives limit the scope of employment contracts and thus reduce their efficiency and productivity in the long run.

After a person has voluntarily entered into any contract, economic conditions may change, so that ex post one wishes he had not accepted the terms of the contract. Suppose that after being hired and after receiving on-the-job training some workers decide to leave their firm. The employer will lose his investment in these workers. That is why firms impose pension penalties on workers who break their contract and leave before retirement.

On the employer side of the contract, when product demand decreases, the firm's demand for labor also decreases. Firms wishing to reduce the size of their work force would like to lay off workers, but under the terms of their contracts they are obliged to retain most workers, especially long-term employees. Some firms struggling to survive may decide to renege on the contract and fire older workers. These firms have concluded that any harm to their reputations is worth the gains from violating their pension and employment contracts. If the risk of adverse economic events and the potential for general layoffs is known to the worker in advance, these risks can be incorporated into the pension contract. Firms with higher risks will have to pay higher wages before workers will want to accept a given defined benefit pension contract. The possibility that failing firms might renege on pensions was one of the reasons for the increase in government regulations.[2]

Other firms have tried to reduce the work force within the terms of the contract by offering special early retirement programs, in other words, by buying the workers out of their contracts. If economic conditions turn out to be worse than anticipated, one cost of long-run employment contracts is that workers are tied to declining industries. In these circumstances, greater mobility would enhance efficiency, but the pension penalty restricts movement. The economic fluctuations of the past fifteen years have helped to shape the debate over pension policy. Greater uncertainty concerning long-run employment prospects will make workers less interested in defined benefit plans and may explain the interest in reducing vesting and participation requirements.

Evolution of Federal Pension Policy

Before 1974, government regulations were primarily concerned with three basic aspects of pensions: the contributions, the range of options, and the benefits. The first regulations were introduced early in the twentieth century when Congress provided preferential tax treatment for pension contributions in an effort to stimulate the growth and development of the private pension system. Under these provisions, firms are allowed to make contributions into pension funds and to treat these contributions as a business expense for corporate tax purposes, even though they still control the pension fund. These contributions are not counted as taxable income to the worker under federal or state income tax laws. Returns on invested pension funds accumulate tax-free until they are disbursed. At retirement, the worker must report realized pension income as taxable income. Employer pension contributions completely escape payroll taxes. This preferential treatment lowers the effective cost of pensions and therefore increases the demand for pension coverage by workers. This favorable tax status was one of the main reasons for the rapid expansion of employer pensions after 1940.

Second, upon taking this step, Congress became more resolved that pensions should be used for the objectives that convinced it to grant this favored tax status in the first place. Thus in 1942 it passed legislation to prevent the tax subsidies from going exclusively to highly paid workers. Specifically, it put limits on the pension benefit that corporate managers could receive relative to the benefits received by production or other lower-wage workers. Although these requirements do not stipulate that all employees must be in the same plan, they do tend to restrict the range of options that firms can offer their workers. In other words, it is difficult to individualize pension plans because comparable tax-qualified plans must be offered to all workers.

Third, in 1974, the government introduced regulations requiring employers to make their pension promises more explicit. Measures were also included to ensure that workers would receive the promised benefits. These regulations specified vesting and participation standards, limits on integration with social security, and funding and investment requirements and made it mandatory to purchase government pension insurance. While these regulations have increased the likelihood that workers will receive their promised benefits, they have also substantially altered how pensions can be used in developing employment contracts.

Much of the recent pension regulation has raised the cost of providing defined benefit plans and, by restricting the terms of the pension contract, reduced the mutual advantages they offer to workers and firms. During the 1980s, the government's pension policy has been greatly influenced by its deficit policy. In an effort to raise additional revenues, Congress has lowered funding limits and put a ceiling on benefits. As a result, plan sponsors now face uncertainties regarding their ability to fund future pension benefits.

The inescapable conclusion is that federal regulation has greatly influenced the course of development of the pension system. By attempting to improve the likelihood that covered workers will receive a future benefit, the government has substantially lowered the gains to workers and firms of adopting defined benefit plans. In this manner, government regulation has stimulated the trend toward defined contribution plans. This trend may result in reduced efficiency and less investment in human capital.

Plan of Analysis

We begin our analysis with a review of the primary characteristics of defined contribution plans (chapter 2) and defined benefit plans (chapter 3), and the incidence of various plan provisions. We then consider the role of pensions as part of implicit, long-run employment contracts and introduce the concept of the pension penalty associated with job changes (chapter 4). Next, we focus on how specific plan provisions affect the magnitude of the pension penalty and the retirement incentives prevalent in most defined benefit plans (chapter 5). Throughout this part of the analysis, we emphasize the role of pensions in personnel policy.

We then turn to the development of the pension system in the United States, focusing first on the growth of pensions and the government policies that influenced pension coverage and plan provisions up to 1974 (chapter 6), and second on the changes since 1974 (chapter 7). We find a sharp increase in the use of defined contribution plans—in all industries and for all plan sizes. Empirical analyses

reveal that only a small portion of the increased use of defined contribution plans can be explained by structural changes in the economy
(chapter 8). After considering other possible explanations, we conclude that the primary reason for the observed changes is the increase
in government regulation.

2
Defined Contribution
Pension Plans

The distinctive feature of a defined contribution pension plan is that part of the worker's compensation consists of contributions made by the employer to a pension account for the worker. The employer's financial liability is limited to these periodic contributions, and there is no promise of a particular benefit at retirement. Workers may also contribute to the pension account, either on a mandatory or a voluntary basis. The pension benefit depends on the lifetime contributions to this account and the rate of return earned on the funds in it. Defined contribution pension plans therefore resemble individual savings accounts, except that they are managed for the worker by the firm or its agent.

The pension plan stipulates the nature of the contributions, which may be a percentage of a worker's salary or a function of the firm's profits, and may include provisions for the firm matching worker contributions up to a certain level. The plan also provides options for investing the funds accrued in the pension account. Typically, there are minimum eligibility requirements for participation in the plan and short vesting periods. In general, workers are eligible to enter such plans if they have less than a year of service or have reached the age of twenty-one. Employer contributions are usually vested fairly quickly; in 1986, for example, vesting was immediate in 26 percent of the savings and thrift plans and 29 percent of deferred profit-sharing plans.[1] Employee contributions are always immediately vested. Thus, the unrestricted ownership of the pension funds quickly falls to the worker. In addition, most defined contribution plans allow departing workers the option of a lump-sum distribution. The value of these funds in defined contribution plans depends on fluctuations in the financial markets.

Data on the characteristics of defined contribution plans used in this analysis are primarily from two sources: (1)BLS, *Employee Benefits in Medium and Large Firms* for the years 1980 to 1986, and (2)the IRS annual 5500 tax reports for primary pension plans with 100 or more participants from 1977 to 1985. ERISA requires that all plans with more than 100 participants file these forms to qualify for preferential tax treatment.

Types of Defined Contribution Plans

Defined contribution plans may be used as supplementary plans, which complement primary defined benefit plans or other defined contribution plans, or as primary plans.[2] The use of defined contribution plans has increased for both primary and supplementary plans. This report concentrates on the increased incidence of primary defined contribution plans. The various types of plans that may qualify for preferential tax treatment under federal regulations include: employee stock-ownership plans (ESOPs), savings and thrift plans, profit-sharing plans, stock-bonus plans, money-purchase plans, and target plans.

Employee stock-ownership plans. In the typical ESOP, the employer transfers a specified contribution into each worker's account and then invests it primarily in company stock. Stock-bonus plans, profit-sharing plans, and money-purchase plans may all be qualified ESOPs if they are entirely funded by the employer and the pension contributions are specified proportions of workers' salaries. ESOPs are more common among professional and administrative employees and technical and clerical workers than among production workers.

Savings and thrift plans. In this case, employees contribute a proportion of their salaries into an account and then select an investment strategy from among several options. Contributions are usually voluntary and workers may have a choice of contribution rates. In 1986 the contribution rates in medium and large firms ranged from 6 to 16 percent of earnings. Employee contributions may be deducted either before or after taxes. Employers may make matching contributions up to a specified limit, which in 1986 was typically 50 percent of the employee's contribution up to the first 6 percent.

Profit-sharing plans. Profit-sharing plans are deferred compensation plans that offer either cash distributions at the end of each year or payment at retirement. Most employees covered by profit-sharing plans are in deferred payment plans that retain the worker's funds until retirement. The employer's contributions are linked to the firm's accumulated or current profits. If employee contributions are required as a condition of employer contributions, the plan is considered a profit-sharing thrift plan. Both types of plans may permit voluntary employee contributions.

Although qualified plans are not required to specify a contribution formula, employers are expected to make recurring and substantial contributions. If a formula is used, it is usually based on a percentage of the firm's profits or a percentage of covered compensation. In 1986, three-fifths of pension participants were in plans that calculated employer contributions by a specified formula, such as a percentage of profits. Others were in plans in which the employers periodically set their own contribution. Small and medium-sized employers often use profit-sharing plans as primary plans. When adopted by large employers, these plans usually supplement existing defined benefit plans.[3]

Stock-bonus plans. Stock-bonus plans are similar to profit-sharing plans except that employer contributions do not depend on profits and retirement benefits are distributed in company stock. Contributions are expressed as a percentage of covered payroll or a percentage of profits.

Money-purchase plans. In money-purchase plans, employer contributions are computed as a percentage of compensation. Employees are usually required to contribute at the same rate as the employer. The contributions are placed in a worker's account, and future retirement benefits are based on the contributions plus accumulated earnings of the fund. The contribution rates are set to yield a desired benefit at retirement.

Target-benefit plans. Although target plans are classified as contribution plans, the contribution rate is linked to a target retirement benefit. To qualify for the projected benefit, each participant must remain with the company until the normal retirement age. Once the required annual contribution necessary to achieve this target benefit is calculated, funds are credited to the employee's account at this rate in each pay period. As in other contribution plans, the actual retirement benefit may be more or less than the target benefit, depending on the investment performance of the funds in the pension account.

Incidence of Defined Contribution Plans

According to the available information on different plan types in use among medium and large firms in 1986, 30 percent of full-time employees were in ESOPs, 28 percent were in savings and thrift plans, and 22 percent were in profit-sharing plans (table 2–1).[4] Professional and administrative workers were more likely to be covered by one of these types. Many employees participated in more than one defined

TABLE 2–1

PERCENTAGE OF FULL-TIME EMPLOYEES PARTICIPATING IN DEFINED
CONTRIBUTION PLANS, 1986

Plan Type	All Employees	Professional and Administrative	Technical and Clerical	Production
Savings and thrift	28	39	36	17
Profit-sharing	22	22	22	22
ESOP	30	32	32	27
Money-purchase	2	2	1	2

SOURCE: U.S. Bureau of Labor Statistics, *Employee Benefits in Medium and Large Firms, 1986*, Bulletin no. 2281, 1987, p. 81.

contribution plan, and 70 percent of participants in defined contribution retirement plans were in plans wholly financed by the employer.[5]

Three-fourths of all defined contribution plans used as primary
pension plans were the profit-sharing type (table 2–2); these plans
covered about 60 percent of all participants in primary defined contribution plans. Money-purchase plans were the next most favored type
of primary defined contribution plan; they covered almost 20 percent
of all participants in primary defined contribution plans in 1985. The
proportion of defined contribution participants who were in money-
purchase plans increased between 1977 and 1985, as did the coverage
rate of stock-bonus plans.

Some analysts have questioned whether it is appropriate to clas-
sify all defined contribution plans as pensions. If individuals can
withdraw funds for other household purposes, should these plans be
called tax-deferred savings plans instead? In 1986, 82 percent of the
participants in savings and thrift plans were allowed to withdraw
some or all of their employers' contributions before the normal payout
at retirement, loss of job due to disability, or terminaton of employment (table 2–3). Twenty-six percent of the participants were in plans
that allowed them to withdraw only in the case of hardships such as
those caused by medical or educational expenses. Withdrawals of
employee contributions made with pre-tax dollars were subject to
Internal Revenue Code provisions governing withdrawal for reasons
of hardship. The options for lump-sum distribution available in many
defined contribution plans increase the chances that funds will be
withdrawn and spent before retirement. Early withdrawals have important implications for the private retirement-income system. If a
substantial proportion of defined contribution plans are merely multi-

purpose, deferred savings plans, the increased use of these plans to replace defined benefit plans could have adverse implications for the retirement income of today's workers.

Risks Associated with Defined Contribution Plans

Defined contribution plans may be considered short-run labor contracts in which negotiated compensation is fully paid to the worker each period. Upon entering such a contract, the worker and firm accept certain financial and labor market risks. To understand why certain groups of workers prefer defined contribution plans to defined benefit plans, one must look at the nature of these risks.

Financial Risks. As already mentioned, the company's financial liability in defined contribution plans ends with the transfer of funds into the worker's account during each pay period. These plans are always fully funded and firms have no residual responsibility con-

---

TABLE 2–2

NUMBER OF PRIMARY DEFINED CONTRIBUTION PLANS AND ACTIVE
PARTICIPANTS, BY PLAN TYPE, 1977 AND 1985

Plan Type	Plans		Participants (millions)	
	1977	1985	1977	1985
Profit-sharing	3,359	9,177	1.5	4.3
	(76.6)	(73.8)	(68.5)	(62.0)
Stock-bonus	288	632	0.3	1.0
	(5.4)	(5.1)	(11.4)	(15.0)
Target-benefit	20	62	0.0	0.0
	(0.5)	(0.5)	(0.6)	(0.3)
Other money-	555	2,236	0.3	1.3
purchase[a]	(12.7)	(18.0)	(12.9)	(19.1)
Other	212	320	0.1	0.2
	(4.8)	(2.6)	(6.4)	(3.5)
Total	4,384	12,427	2.2	6.96
	(100.0)	(100.0)	(100.0)	(100.0)

NOTE: Firms with no primary plans of 100 or more participants and tax-exempt organizations are excluded. The numbers in parentheses represent percentage of column totals.
a. All money-purchase plans that do not have a target benefit.
SOURCE: Calculations from 1977 and 1985 5500 Reporting Forms.

TABLE 2–3

PERCENTAGE OF PARTICIPANTS IN SAVINGS AND THRIFT PLANS WITH
PROVISIONS FOR WITHDRAWAL OF EMPLOYER CONTRIBUTIONS
BEFORE NORMAL PAYOUT, 1986

Least Restrictive Provisions	All Participants
Withdrawals permitted	82
For hardship reasons	26
No penalty	21
Penalty	5
For any reason	56
No penalty	19
Penalty	37
No withdrawals permitted	18
Total	100

NOTE: Normal payout typically occurs at retirement, retirement because of disability, or termination of employment.
SOURCE: U.S. Bureau of Labor Statistics, *Employee Benefits in Medium and Large Firms, 1986*, Bulletin no. 2281, 1987, p. 85.

cerning future benefits. Because the retirement benefit depends on the size of the pension fund when it is withdrawn, plan participants bear all the financial risks associated with the rate of return on the fund. Low returns throughout one's work life produce a low retirement benefit, whereas higher interest rates or increases in equity prices produce a larger benefit at retirement. The retirement benefit relative to preretirement earnings or the replacement ratio is uncertain. If the contribution rate and the rate of return are held constant, workers with more rapidly increasing earnings will have lower replacement ratios. Of course, lower rates of return will also yield lower replacement rates.

Participants must decide how much financial risk they are willing to accept. Most plans offer several investment options with different risks and associated rates of return. In general, these choices are similar to those faced by any investor, except that the worker may have little control over the termination of the investment. In some plans, workers are required to liquidate their holdings in the pension fund when they leave the company, whether or not it is the best time to sell these assets. Major changes in work life (such as retirement, quitting, or a layoff) do not often coincide with peaks in the value of one's pension fund. The fact that the timing of work decisions may affect the pension received increases the financial risks associated with defined contribution plans.

This risk is somewhat offset, however, if the worker has a say in the composition of the pension fund portfolio. For example, by being able to switch from equities into assets that are less volatile, the worker can reduce the risks associated with the timing of retirement. As financial markets have matured, investors have gained more options by which to diversify risks, and many defined contribution plans now offer some of these options. Under federal pension regulations adopted recently, defined contribution plans must offer their participants a minimum set of investment options, and these options must vary with respect to their risk and expected rate of return.

Some defined contribution plans carry firm-specific risks. In profit-sharing plans, the rate of contribution is directly linked to the short-run financial success of the company. Thus, total lifetime pension contributions depend on the well-being of the individual company. Similarly, the value of pension funds for participants in ESOPs is directly linked to the market price of the company's stock. Fluctuations in the price of this one company will affect the retirement funds of its employees.

Labor Market Risks. Inasmuch as participants in defined contribution plans are allowed to own the rights to the funds in their pension accounts, usually after only a brief period of employment, these funds are considered their property and will remain so whether they continue to be employed by the company or decide to change jobs. Thus, the value of the pension account does not depend on the decision to remain on the job. Of course, future accumulations depend on the pensions offered by the current employer and by prospective employers. Also, participants in these plans do not incur any loss in accumulated pension wealth if they are laid off or if the firm goes bankrupt (provided that pension funds are not invested in company stock).

These ownership rights to the pension fund mean that there is little or no risk of losing pension wealth when changing employers. Some firms allow a worker to receive a lump sum as soon as the job terminates, and to move these funds into a new pension account. Defined contribution funds are therefore portable.

Participation in these plans should not affect worker decisions to change jobs or retire. These pensions represent additional employment compensation, but do not offer employees any special incentives to alter their labor market decisions. They do not impose any systematic costs on workers who quit the firm early and do not provide financial incentives to retire early. Contributions into defined contribution plans represent current compensation for current work and are treated like cash earnings.

Inflation Risk. If unanticipated inflation occurs before retirement, real returns on pension investments change. To the extent that nominal returns rise to reflect price increases, the worker's pension wealth is protected against uncertain inflation. How returns respond to price changes will depend on the choice of investments. Pension wealth continues to grow when workers quit pension-covered jobs but leave their pension wealth in their previous employers' plans. Whether pension wealth declines in real terms with rising prices depends on the sensitivity of the investment to inflation.

Inflation after retirement will lower pension wealth if the worker has selected a fixed annuity option, that is, if the value in the pension account has been converted to a fixed annuity. In this case, the worker cannot expect postretirement benefits to increase; rather, the real value of pension benefits will decline as prices increase. Variable annuities, like those pioneered by Teachers' Insurance Annuity Association offer some protection against inflation because the benefit is based on continuing equity investments. The retiree can also select a lump-sum disbursement, invest these funds, and use the returns as a form of pension income. In this strategy, the relationship between inflation and the rate of return on the investment will determine how real retirement income responds to rising prices.

Defined Contribution Plans and Employment Contracts

In a defined contribution plan, the pension compensation—or the accrued cost to the employer—is exactly equal to the employer contribution. The company transfers a predetermined amount—usually specified as a percentage of earnings—into the pension account of workers each pay period. This percentage typically is not a function of age or job tenure, and does not vary with the level of earnings unless the plan is integrated with social security (in which case the percentage of earnings contributed by the firm may increase above some designated level of monthly earnings).

The annual earnings and pension compensation during the lifetime of a hypothetical worker are shown in table 2–4. This worker is assumed to be hired at age twenty-five, starting at $15,000 per year. The firm contributes 7.5 percent of this annual compensation (or $1,047 at age twenty-five) into a defined contribution plan on behalf of the worker. Therefore the worker has cash earnings of $13,953 at age twenty-five. The worker remains with the firm until retirement, and over the years total compensation increases by 6 percent. Consequently, both cash earnings and pension compensation increased 6 percent per year. The rate of return on invested pension funds is assumed to be 6 percent per year. In this plan, the worker could retire at any time after age sixty and receive a lump-sum distribution, or the company would convert the pension fund into a life annuity for the worker. Alternatively, the worker could quit at any time and receive a lump-sum distribution equal to the accumulated pension wealth.

In this example salary and pension compensation increase at the same rate throughout the work life (since pension compensation is fixed at 7.5 percent of salary). The value of the pension fund increases annually as a result of additional firm contributions and the 6 percent rate of return on the existing funds in the worker's account. Thus, each year the fund increases by 6 percent of its value in the previous year plus pension compensation equal to 7.5 percent of the workers' cash earnings.

Since the worker owns these funds, their value does not depend

TABLE 2–4

COMPENSATION PROFILE FOR A HYPOTHETICAL WORKER IN
A DEFINED CONTRIBUTION PLAN
(dollars)

Age	Tenure	Earnings	Pension Compensation	Pension Contribution Rate (percent)	Nominal Pension Wealth	Real Pension Wealth[a]
25	0	13,953	1,047	7.5	0	0
30	5	18,743	1,406	7.5	6,616	6,135
35	10	25,178	1,888	7.5	17,741	15,016
40	15	33,821	2,537	7.5	35,679	27,650
45	20	45,431	3,407	7.5	63,783	45,399
50	25	61,027	4,577	7.5	106,896	70,100
55	30	81,976	6,148	7.5	171,987	104,231
60	35	110,117	8,259	7.5	269,026	151,125
65	40	147,919	11,094	7.5	412,229	215,274

a. Nominal pension wealth deflated back to dollars at twenty-five.
SOURCE: Simulation is based on a worker hired by firm at age twenty-five and receiving total compensation of $15,000. Worker is covered by a defined contribution plan that requires the employer to contribute 7.5 percent of salary annually into the pension account.

on actual or expected job changes. For example, if the worker changed jobs every ten years, moving to employers who offered the same cash earnings and the same pension plan, the lifetime profiles of earnings, pension compensation, and pension wealth would not be affected by the job changes. Pension wealth is the value of the pension fund at each successive point in time.

To reiterate, in a defined contribution plan the employer is required to contribute a fixed amount to a pension account for the employee at the end of each pay period. Whether the worker remains with the same company or switches jobs has no bearing on the value of the funds in this account. The contribution rate is generally the same for workers of all ages. As a result, defined contribution pension plans represent current compensation in exchange for current work. The value of retirement benefits based on work to date is not contingent on future work performance of the plan participant. Thus, these plans cannot be used as part of implicit contracts that attempt to modify worker performance and behavior by making a future payment contingent on work activities prior to retirement.

In this framework, an economic model of defined contribution plans would specify that each period workers are paid in cash earnings, pension contributions, and other fringe benefits. Since defined contribution plans do not alter worker behavior, firms should be viewed as neutral sellers of pensions. This means that firms will sell a dollar of pension compensation for a dollar reduction in earnings. Workers are willing to accept these terms because of the preferential tax treatment accorded employer pension contributions. Workers covered by these plans should exhibit the same quit and retirement patterns as those not covered by pensions. These pensions are not expected to alter productivity, effort, or investments in human capital. In general, the behavior of participants of defined contribution plans should be more like the behavior of workers not covered by a pension than that of participants in defined benefit plans.

3
Defined Benefit Pension Plans

A distinctive feature of defined benefit plans is their structural diversity. Plan provisions may vary across firms and a particular benefit formula may yield substantially different benefits to workers in the same firm. Therefore it is considerably more difficult to evaluate pension compensation and pension wealth in these plans than in defined contribution plans. Another notable difference is that defined benefit plans specify the benefit that employers promise to pay their workers at retirement; generally, the amount is based on years of service and earnings as well as vesting and portability provisions. Frequently, only final earnings are included in the benefit formula. As a result, pension wealth in defined benefit plans is a function of the frequency of job changes and the age of retirement.

Provisions of Defined Benefit Plans

The value of pension benefits is determined by a number of factors: the benefit formula itself, social security integration, maximum benefit provisions, retirement ages, the continuation of wage and service accruals, vesting and portability standards, and postretirement increases.

Benefit Formula. There are two basic types of benefit formulas: one is based on earnings and the other on a specified dollar amount. The former is the type most frequently used.

Earnings formula. The benefit according to this formula is calculated by multiplying a generosity parameter times years of service times average earnings—for example, 1.5 percent of earnings per year of service. The proportion of participants covered by earnings formulas has remained relatively stable during the 1980s (table 3–1). In 1986, 57 percent of all participants in defined benefit plans were covered by an earnings formula based on the *final working years*. The averaging period was generally five years. Of participants covered by final earnings formulas, 84 percent were in plans based on earnings in

TABLE 3–1

DISTRIBUTION OF BENEFIT FORMULAS IN DEFINED BENEFIT PLANS,
1980–1986
(percent)

Formula Type	1980	1982	1984	1986
Terminal-earnings	53	52	54	57
Career-earnings	15	15	14	15
Dollar-amount	30	30	28	26
Other formulas	2	3	4	1

NOTE: Entries represent the proportion of participants in defined benefit plans covered by each formula type. Because of rounding, sums of individual items may not equal totals.
SOURCE: U.S. Bureau of Labor Statistics, *Employee Benefits Survey of Medium and Large Firms*, various years.

the last or high five years, and the remainder were in plans using the last or high three years of earnings.[1]

Another 15 percent of the participants in defined benefit plans in 1986 were covered by *career-earnings formulas*.[2] In these plans, benefits are based on the average of all earnings during the worker's career with the firm. Since a worker's earnings typically rise over time, career-earnings plans yield a lower benefit than terminal-earnings plans with the same benefit formula. This difference is even greater during periods of high inflation. In recent years, career-earnings plans have become less common. During the late 1960s and the 1970s, many plans were amended to reduce the number of years included in the earnings averaging period in response to high rates of inflation.

Dollar-amount formula. This formula calculates benefits as a flat dollar amount times years of service, or simply a specified dollar amount to all qualified retirees. It was used in plans covering 26 percent of all the participants in defined benefit plans in 1986. This formula is more frequently used in plans that are collectively bargained as it provides a means of reducing the variance in benefits across retirees. Thus, across a cohort of retirees, benefits will be more equally distributed than were the earnings of the cohort.[3] The benefit amounts in this case are regularly increased through contract negotiations, usually between the firm and the union. Benefit increases tend to keep pace with earnings over time, so that replacement ratios remain relatively constant from one group of retirees to another.

Social Security Integration. Firms are permitted to consider the employer's social security retirement contributions or the worker's social security benefit in developing pension benefit formulas. Almost two-thirds of the defined benefit plan participants in 1986 had their pension benefits integrated with social security benefits; the proportion increased from 45 percent in 1980 to 62 percent in 1986 (see table 3–2). Smaller plans are more likely to be integrated than larger plans.[4] Integration provisions cover 90 percent of participants in terminal-earnings plans, but only 69 percent of participants in career-earnings plans. Integration is virtually nonexistent among participants in dollar-amount plans.[5]

The Internal Revenue Code allows qualified pension plans to employ two types of integration: the excess method and the offset method. Firms using the excess method base a greater percentage of benefits on earnings above the social security taxable earnings limit than on earnings below this limit. Until 1988, pension benefits based on earnings above the specified limit could not exceed 1.4 percent per year of service, or a total of 37.5 percent of plan benefits based on earnings below that level. This results in a more generous benefit formula for earnings above the earnings limit specified in the plan.

Plans could not set the integration level of earnings higher than the social security taxable earnings limit in the current year. Most plans set the limit well below the allowable amount and tended not to increase it as the social security earnings limit rose.[6] In 1989, the integration limits were reduced to 0.75 of a percentage point per year of service and a maximum of 26.25 percentage points. In 1986, the

TABLE 3–2

PROPORTION OF PARTICIPANTS IN DEFINED BENEFIT PLANS USING INTEGRATION FORMULAS, 1980–1986

(percent)

Integration	1980	1982	1984	1986
With integrated formula	45	45	56	62
Offset method	30	35	36	43
Excess method	16	10	20	24
Without integrated formula	55	55	44	38

NOTE: Because of rounding, sums of individual items may not equal totals. In addition, some plans have more than one benefit formula and the alternative formulas may use different integration methods. Such plans are included as using both types of integration methods.

SOURCE: U.S. Bureau of Labor Statistics, *Employee Benefits Survey of Medium and Large Firms*, various years.

excess method of integration was used for 24 percent of all participants in defined benefit plans.

The offset method allows the firm to subtract a specified portion of the retiree's social security primary insurance amount (PIA) from the pension benefit. Before 1988, the offset could not exceed 83.33 percent of the worker's PIA. Most surveys indicate that integrated plans do not use the maximum possible offsets. Most offset plans use 50 percent of the PIA. Offset provisions covered 43 percent of the participants in defined benefit plans in 1986. Under new regulations introduced in 1988, the offset cannot reduce the original pension benefit by more than half and may not be more than 0.75 percent of the final average pay for each year of plan service.

Social security integration has created considerable controversy as its use systematically reduces the benefits of the lowest-wage workers more than integration reduces the benefits of high-wage workers. The rationale for this approach is that social security benefits are a form of retirement benefits and should be taken into account in determining the acceptable limits on benefits. Without integration, a pension that provides an acceptable replacement ratio to high-income workers would provide some low-wage workers with total income replacement ratios (pension plus social security) of more than 100 percent. Since social security, like an employer pension, is financed by worker and firm payments, the government has allowed the two to be integrated in order to achieve a desirable total replacement ratio.

Maximum-Benefit Provisions. Some pension plans set a limit on the pension benefit that any worker can achieve. In 1986, 41 percent of the participants in defined benefit pension plans were covered by a maximum benefit provision. Such provisions are much more common in terminal-earnings plans. Fifty-six percent of all participants in such plans were covered by benefit limits. In contrast, only 8 percent of the participants in career-earnings plans and 26 percent of participants in dollar-amount plans were covered by maximum-benefit provisions.

In most cases, benefits are capped by limiting the years of credited service that can be included in the benefit formula. Table 3–3 shows the proportion of participants covered by maximum-benefit provisions in 1986 and the maximum number of years permitted in determining the benefit amount: 36 percent of the participants in defined benefit plans were covered by formulas that put a limit on the number of years of credited service, usually thirty or thirty-five years; and 7 percent were in plans that set a maximum percentage of terminal or career earnings or a maximum dollar amount.

One objective of maximum-benefit provisions is to ensure that retirement benefits do not exceed earnings from work. Another is to encourage long-tenured workers to retire. When a worker reaches the benefit limit, pension compensation falls because pension accruals are stopped. Therefore, the gain from continued work declines sharply. By using maximum-benefit provisions to retire their older workers, employers are able to achieve the desired age distribution of their labor force.

Retirement Ages. Defined benefit plans specify an age at which workers can normally retire without a reduction in benefits. At this age, benefits are calculated by the formula stated in the plan. The normal retirement age may or may not be linked to years of service. In recent years, the age of normal retirement has been lowered in many plans. In 1986 only 36 percent of participants were in plans with sixty-five as the normal retirement age, 19 percent were in plans with retirement at age sixty-two, and 14 percent were in plans with retire-

TABLE 3–3

DISTRIBUTION OF MAXIMUM-BENEFIT PROVISIONS IN
DEFINED BENEFIT PLANS, 1986
(percent)

| | | Formula Type (percentage of participants) | | |
Benefit Limits	Total	Final-earnings	Career-earnings	Dollar-amount
With maximum benefit	41	56	8	26
Limits years of credited				
service[a]	36	50	8	20
20 years	1	2	0	1
25 years	5	5	0	4
30 years	12	17	1	7
35 years	9	14	0	2
40 years	6	8	4	2
more than 40 years	1	1	2	1
Other maximum[b]	7	9	0	9
Not subject to maximum	59	44	92	74

a. Some limits with small frequencies have been omitted.
b. The benefit yielded under the formula is limited to either a percentage of terminal or career earnings or to a flat dollar amount.
SOURCE: U.S. Bureau of Labor Statistics, *Employee Benefits in Medium and Large Firms, 1986*, Bulletin no. 2281, 1987, p. 66.

ment at sixty. Eleven percent of the participants were in plans that used a criterion of age plus service, which in most cases totaled eighty-five or ninety for normal retirement. Another 13 percent were in plans that had no age requirement, so workers could retire without penalty with thirty years of service.

Virtually all participants in defined benefit plans (98 percent) have early retirement options, although there is usually an age and service requirement (most commonly age fifty-five with ten years of service). In general, early retirement benefits are calculated by applying a reduction factor to the benefit formula used to determine the normal retirement benefit. The reduction factor may be a constant for each year taken before the normal retirement age, or it may vary by age. In most cases, reductions in benefits at early retirement are less than the required actuarial adjustment that would equate the wealth value of the pension at early and normal retirement.

Retirement age provisions influence the retirement behavior of older workers in several ways. First, as soon as benefits become available, workers have an incentive to retire or simply leave the firm. Second, after they pass the age of eligibility for benefits, most workers obtain lower gains from continued work because they must now forgo a year's benefit to remain on the job. Thus, firms and workers usually pay close attention to the implications of early and normal retirement. The ages involved can be used as part of the employment contract to alter worker behavior and reduce firm costs. Third, early retirement options may be used to increase the rate of early retirement. (The effect of early retirement on pension compensation and pension wealth is discussed in chapter 4.)

Wage and Service Accruals Past Normal Retirement. Prior to legislation enacted in 1986, pension plans were allowed to stop crediting wage and service accruals after the normal retirement age. If accruals are stopped, pension benefits are frozen when the worker reaches the age of normal retirement. This causes a sharp decline in pension compensation. To remain on the job, workers must forgo a year's benefits, and without additional accruals the benefit payable next year will be the same as the one not taken. Therefore, pension compensation is negative and equal to the benefit forgone by remaining on the job. As a result, pension wealth declines with continued work and workers have a strong incentive to retire at or before the normal retirement age.

In 1986, 59 percent of participants were covered by some type of provision that ceased to credit service after age sixty-five (table 3–4); 51 percent of all participants were covered by plans that stopped crediting service and deferred the pension with no change in the benefit amount. Workers in such plans must forgo a year's benefit to continue working, with no subsequent increase in benefits. Another 18 percent of participants were in plans that credited service after age sixty-five, subject to a maximum-age restriction.

Interestingly, defined benefit plans can be designed with few retirement incentives. This can be done by granting wage and service accruals and by awarding actuarial increases (similar to reductions for early retirement) for work beyond the normal retirement age. In 1986, only 1 percent of participants were in plans of this type. Retirement incentives can also be reduced by allowing the benefits to begin at the normal retirement age even though employees remain on the job.

Under legislation enacted in 1986, defined benefit plans are required to award wage and service accruals as long as workers remain

TABLE 3–4

DISTRIBUTION OF PARTICIPANTS IN PLANS LIMITING CREDIT FOR SERVICE AFTER AGE SIXTY-FIVE, 1986

(percent)

Type of Credit	All Participants	Professional and Administrative	Technical and Clerical	Production
No credit for service	59	59	66	55
Pension deferred with no change in amount	51	52	55	49
Pension deferred but increased actuarially	5	5	6	5
Pension deferred but increased each additional year	2	2	3	1
Pension begins at 65	1	0	1	1
Credit for service, no actuarial increase	40	39	34	44
All service credited	22	23	21	21
All service credited to specific age	18	16	12	23
Credit for service with actuarial increase for later retirement	1	1	1	1

SOURCE: U.S. Bureau of Labor Statistics, *Employee Benefits in Medium and Large Firms, 1986*, Bulletin no. 2281, 1987, p. 71.

on the job. Although this regulation eliminates one of the retirement incentives for older workers, a number of other strategies can be used to achieve the same effect.

Vesting and Portability. Vesting means conveying to the worker the right to claim whatever pension benefit he is legally entitled to upon leaving the firm. If the worker leaves before being vested, he will receive no retirement benefits. Up to 1989, firms were allowed to select one of three vesting rules: 100 percent vesting of accrued benefits after ten years of service; 25 percent vesting of accrued benefits after five years of service, with additional vesting accruing each year until the worker is 100 percent vested after fifteen years; and 50 percent vesting of accrued benefits when age and service add to forty-five, with 100 percent vesting five years later. In 1986, almost 90 percent of participants in defined benefit plans were covered by ten-year vesting rules. Legislation enacted in 1986 altered vesting standards, beginning in 1989. Workers must now be either 100 percent vested after five years or 20 percent vested after three years and 100 percent after seven years. Most firms will no doubt adopt the 100 percent five-year vesting option for the same reasons they previously selected ten-year vesting: It is simpler to administer and easier to explain to workers.

Even under 100 percent vesting, workers are penalized if they leave the firm before retirement. The penalty depends on plan provisions concerning the benefit formula, vesting standards, and the portability of pension credits from one plan to another (see chapters 4 and 5). For example, workers in a multi-employer pension plan can move from one firm to another in the plan and have all years of work credited toward a single pension. Thus, their service credits are portable among the firms in the plan. There is no comparable portability among single-employer pensions. The size of this loss depends on the benefit formula; final-average formulas produce a much larger loss than career-average formulas. Without this portability, job-changers who are in defined benefit plans will have lower lifetime pension wealth than single-career workers. This pension penalty is what enforces the implicit pension contract and thereby reduces mobility and enhances productivity.

Postretirement Benefit Increases. The lifetime value of pension benefits depends on inflation and the subsequent response of pension benefits. When inflation is not matched by benefit increases, the real value of the pension decreases. Until recently, it was widely believed that pension benefits were fixed in nominal terms at retirement. Surveys of large firms indicate that less than 5 percent of private plans automatically increase benefits in response to inflation.

The lack of automatic adjustments, however, does not necessarily imply that no postretirement increases are granted. During the second half of the 1970s, approximately two-thirds of large plans provided one or more ad hoc increases.[7] Between 1973 and 1979, when the Consumer Price Index rose by 63 percent, average benefits for persons already retired in 1973 increased by 24 percent.[8] In 1986, 46 percent of all participants were in plans that awarded at least one increase between 1981 and 1985. This is somewhat lower than the proportion of participants in plans that were granting increases during the years of high inflation in the late 1970s. Although ad hoc benefit increases appear to be frequent and widespread, they are not sufficient to maintain the real value of pension benefits. Benefit increases are more frequent and larger in collectively bargained plans[9] and in large plans.[10]

Average Plan Provisions in Defined Benefit Plans. To illustrate the diversity of defined benefit plans, we have derived average plan provisions that prevailed in 1983 in various industries and occupations, and firms of different sizes, as shown in table 3–5. The benefit formula shown for each group (which may be based on earnings, dollars per year of service, or a fixed dollar amount) is the type most frequently used in that group. The formula parameters and eligibility requirements are based on group means.

Plan provisions differ across industry, by occupation within industry, and by firm size within industry and occupation. For example, in manufacturing and wholesale trade, professional and administrative workers as well as technical and clerical workers are covered by formulas based on earnings, whereas production workers are covered by formulas based on dollars per year of service. Among production workers in manufacturing, pension accruals per year of service and eligibility requirements vary by firm size. Workers in large firms earn $190 for every year of service and become eligible for full benefits after thirty years of service, whereas workers in small firms (less than 1,000 workers) earn $134 for each year of service and can receive benefits at age sixty-five regardless of years of service. The most common plan is a terminal-earnings formula based on the last five years' earnings. Even among these plans, the generosity parameter varies by industry, occupation, and firm size.[11]

TABLE 3–5
TYPICAL DEFINED BENEFIT PENSION FORMULAS BY INDUSTRY, OCCUPATION, AND FIRM SIZE

Group by Industry, Occupation, and Size	Benefit Formula[a]	Salary Averaging Period (years)	Eligibility Requirements[b]		
Mining					
Professional and administrative	1.58% × S × Y	4	61	+	12 Y
Technical and clerical	1.60% × S × Y	4	61	+	12 Y
Production	1.47% × S × Y	3	Age	+	Y=78
Construction	1.50% × S × Y (S≤10,800) + 2.00% × S × Y (excess)	career	64	+	10 Y
Manufacturing					
Professional and administrative					
<1,000 employees	1.54% × S × Y	5	64		
1,000+ employees	1.53% × S × Y	5	59	+	19 Y
Technical and clerical					
<1,000 employees	1.58% × S × Y	5	64		
1,000+ employees	1.51% × S × Y	5	Age	+	Y=78
Production					
<1,000 employees	$134.04 × Y		65		
1,000+ employees	$190.08 × Y		30 Y		
Transportation and communications					
Professional and administrative					
<1,000 employees	1.81% × S × Y (S≤10,380) + 1.85% × S × Y (excess)	5	Age	+	Y=76

		career	
1,000 + employees	$1.60\% \times S \times Y$		Age + Y=76
Technical and clerical			
<1,000 employees	$1.67\% \times S \times Y$	5	Age + Y=76
1,000 + employees	$\$162.96 \times Y +$ $1.38\% \times S \times Y\ (S>\$12,128)$	3	30 Y
Production			
<1,000 employees	$1.63\% \times S \times Y$	5	Age + Y=76
1,000 + employees	$\$163.93 \times Y +$ $1.37\% \times S \times Y\ (S>\$12,351)$	3	30 Y
Wholesale trade			
Professional and administrative	$1.60\% \times S \times Y$	4	61 + 17Y
Technical and clerical	$1.57\% \times S \times Y$	4	64
Production	$\$197.76 \times Y$		60 + 15 Y
Retail trade			
Professional and administrative			
<1,000 employees	$1.28\% \times S \times Y$	5	65
1,000 + employees	$1.66\% \times S \times Y$	5	64
Technical and clerical			
<1,000 employees	$1.20\% \times S \times Y$	5	63
1,000 + employees	$1.50\% \times S \times Y$ (to age 50) + $2.00\% \times S \times Y$ (after age 50)	5	64
Production			
<1,000 employees	$1.23\% \times S \times Y$	5	65
1,000 + employees	$1.50\% \times S \times Y$	5	64

(Table continues)

TABLE 3–5 (continued)

Group by Industry, Occupation, and Size	Benefit Formula[a]	Salary Averaging Period (years)	Eligibility Requirements[b]
Finance, insurance, and real estate			
Professional and administrative			
<1,000 employees	$1.88\% \times S \times Y$	5	64
1,000+ employees	$1.79\% \times S \times Y$	5	63
Technical & clerical			
<1,000 employees	$1.85\% \times S \times Y$	5	65
1,000+ employees	$1.77\% \times S \times Y$	5	63
Production			
<1,000 employees	$2.04\% \times S \times Y$	4	64
1,000+ employees	$1.06\% \times S \times Y$ (S≤SS base) + $1.61\% \times S \times Y$ (excess)	5	61 + 24 Y
Services			
Professional and administrative	$1.54\% \times S \times Y$	5	65
Technical and clerical	$0.94\% \times S \times Y$ (S≤SS base) + $1.63\% \times S \times Y$ (excess)	career	65
Production	$1.46\% \times S \times Y$ (S≤8,576) + $2.40\% \times S \times Y$ (excess)	career	62 + 10 Y

a. These formulas define annual benefits at retirement; S is the average salary, Y is years of service, and SS base is the social security earnings limit.

b. The first figure represents retirement age and the second required years of service.

SOURCE: U.S. Bureau of Labor Statistics Employee Benefits Survey of Medium and Large Firms, 1983.

Risks Associated with Defined Benefit Plans

Defined benefit plans promise workers a retirement benefit that is a function of years of service and earnings. It is not directly related to contributions or the value of the pension fund. The firm and not the worker is the owner of the pension fund, and it is the firm's responsibility to pay the promised benefit. These concepts differ from those underlying defined contribution plans. Therefore, the risks also differ.

Financial Risks. Participants in defined benefit plans do not bear directly the risk of cyclical fluctuations in the actual rate of return on invested pension funds. The firm is responsible for providing sufficient funds to pay the promised benefits. The expected cost of the plan is based on an anticipated long-run rate of return. Periodically, the firm transfers money into the pension fund, and is obliged to put in additional money if the fund does not contain enough to pay the promised benefit. Rates of return higher than those projected allow firms to reduce their contributions, whereas below-average returns force the firm to make additional contributions.

The burden of the financial risks associated with a defined benefit plan can be illustrated by considering a worker nearing retirement age. Suppose that the value of the assets in the person's pension fund drops because of a decline in equity prices. Such a change would not affect the retirement benefit of the person in a defined benefit plan. In contrast, an older worker covered by a defined contribution plan would be facing the prospect of a reduced retirement annuity. Unlike cyclical fluctuations in rates of return, long-run changes in rates of return will be reflected in the long-run cost of the plan. In the long run, workers pay for their pension by accepting lower wages. Therefore, changes in the long-run pension cost will be passed on to workers in the form of lower future wages.

The employee's increased certainty about the benefit amount is partly the reason for the greater use of defined benefit plans. Workers who are averse to the risks associated with financial market fluctuations prefer defined benefit plans, particularly since such risks may make retirement planning more difficult. A longer time horizon makes firms more willing to bear the short-run financial risks involved in pensions.[12]

Labor Market Risks. If lifetime earnings are held constant, workers in defined benefit plans who change jobs will accumulate lower lifetime benefits than workers who remain with a single employer. This follows from benefit formulas, vesting periods, and the lack of portability across plans. The pension penalties associated with mobility

31

in defined benefit plans create labor market risks that are likely to induce more mobile workers to prefer defined contribution plans. An example would be workers in small businesses, who tend to have higher turnover rates than similar workers in large corporations. Another factor to consider is that small firms are more likely to go bankrupt[13] and thus impose a pension loss on workers. The loss will occur even if the pension plan is fully funded, because the worker will not be able to continue to accumulate pension credits by remaining on the job. A plant closing thus has the same effect as a voluntary job change. Moreover, if there are insufficient assets to pay the promised benefits and the firm goes into bankruptcy, pension losses will be all the greater. The Pension Benefit Guaranty Corporation has been established to safeguard against this latter risk. Not surprisingly, workers in small firms are more likely to be covered by defined contribution plans, and lower quit rates are found among unionized workers, who tend to prefer defined benefit plans.

If the cost of hiring or training workers is high, a firm will use its total compensation package to try to keep its workers. Defined benefit pension plans are one way to reduce the turnover rate. Lower turnover rates can benefit workers if they lead the firm to invest more in training and higher total compensations.

Inflation Risks. The pension loss suffered by participants who leave jobs before retirement is a function of inflation. Vested benefits in a defined benefit plan are frozen in nominal terms at the time of job termination. This means that price increases between the time of job separation and retirement reduce the real value of the benefits in retirement. Thus, workers who have changed jobs bear all the risk of inflation during this interval.

In contrast, the firm bears the inflation risk for workers who remain on the job. As cash earnings rise to reflect higher prices, future pension benefits also rise. Under final-earnings plans, real future pension benefits are not eroded by price increases if wages keep up with inflation. Firms must provide the required contributions to fund real pension benefits for workers remaining with their employers until retirement. Career-earnings plans provide less protection against inflation.

Inflation after retirement will reduce the real value of pension benefits unless the benefits are raised at the same rate as inflation. Private pensions seldom use this approach. Most pensions provide irregular partial adjustment of benefits. Benefits are usually increased at the discretion of the employer. Thus, workers bear most of the risk of postretirement inflation.

4
Pensions and Employment Contracts

Two theories have been proposed to explain the nature of the defined benefit pension contract between workers and firms. Both theories take into account how workers pay for their pensions, but differ in their predictions about the shape of the earnings profile and the pension incentives for workers to remain with their employers. Numerical simulation methods have been developed to illustrate how different plan characteristics and savings methods affect earnings profiles. The results provide insight into the magnitude of incentives for workers at various ages during their working careers.

Employment Contracts, Efficiency, and Compensation

The fundamental principle of wage theory in a competitive market is that workers are compensated in accordance with their value to the firm, as measured by their marginal product. Compensation includes cash earnings and pensions, as well as other employee benefits. In a world without risk or information costs, compensation per period should equal the marginal product of the worker. In a life cycle context, the worker is viewed as entering the labor market with a specific level of productivity. This initial productivity is determined by the value of existing skills, which may be augmented over time by further training. The time devoted to training and to acquiring new skills is expected to be relatively large early in life, to decline as the worker ages, and perhaps to stop some time before retirement. Of course, skills may depreciate with time, and if the rate of depreciation exceeds the rate of new investment, productivity and earnings will decline.

Accordingly, human capital models[1] predict that earnings are relatively low early in life, rise throughout most of a person's work life, and then level off during the final working years. Workers with similar initial skills and similar patterns of investment are expected to have similar earnings profiles throughout their work lives. Earnings will be equal to marginal productivity if all skills represent general human capital. General human capital refers to skills that are valued by many firms. Because these skills are useful at many firms, many employers are willing to base wages on general human capital.

Other employers are more interested in specific human capital, which refers to the skills needed to enhance productivity at a particular firm. Workers with some firm-financed, specific human capital will be paid less than their marginal productivity at their current employer; however, this wage will exceed wage offers from other firms that are based only on the worker's general human capital. Firms have no incentive to lay off older workers or to reduce their wages dramatically except as productivity declines. Firms may attempt to reduce turnover rates and related training costs by sharing with workers some of the returns to specific training in the form of increased cash earnings or promises of future pension benefits.

Implicit Lifetime Contracts. Researchers have found most workers remain with a single employer for many years and that those with more years of service with a single firm have higher earnings than otherwise identical workers.[2] According to the theory of implicit contracts, workers and firms enter into this quasi-permanent relationship because it benefits both parties. Firms offer workers lifetime compensation that is structured to pay them less than their productivity earlier in their careers and overpay them in their final working years. These contracts are designed to limit the turnover of employees and to motivate them to produce more. For example, if a job requires firm-specific skills, employment agreements may defer compensation to discourage the workers from quitting and taking their specific capital with them. Of course, if the promise is to be meaningful, workers must be protected from future wage reductions and layoffs or be compensated for these risks.

Some economists argue that such contracts have come into being because monitoring costs are too high to review workers' output constantly.[3] If the rate of pay is established at the beginning of a contract period and workers are evaluated only at discrete intervals, they may not exert the agreed-upon level of effort. To encourage workers to perform at appropriate levels of effort, firms pay less than their productivity during their earlier working years, but promise that compensation will exceed productivity in later years. If such a deferral arrangement is beneficial to workers, they will agree to it.

Assume that the worker enters the labor market with productivity $P(H)$, where productivity (P) is a function of a high level of effort

(H), and does nothing to augment this stock throughout his work life, so that productivity at retirement is also *P(H)*. This level of productivity can be achieved only if the worker exerts a high level of effort *(H)*, which implies greater disutility from working than from a lower level of effort *(L)*. However, a lower level of effort yields a realized productivity of *P(L)*.

In a labor market where contracting and payment occur at the beginning of the period but effort is observed only at the end of the period, firms will agree to pay only at the lower level of effort. Consider the alternative. A firm contracts for a higher level of effort and sets $W = P(H)$. The worker accepts the contract and then performs at the lower level of effort. At the end of the period, the worker is found to have failed to meet the terms of the contract and is not rehired. Upon termination, the worker sells his services to another firm that will contract with him only at the rate it pays for a lower level of effort because of his reputation. The initial employer has suffered an economic loss by paying a wage in excess of the actual contribution of the worker. Therefore, if contracts are limited to a single period, firms will not be willing to pay compensation higher than $W = P(L)$.

Under a lifetime contract, workers agree to be paid less than their productivity in the early working years in return for a promise that if they provide the higher level of effort they will be retained and paid in excess of their productivity in the final working years. Therefore, the earnings profile increases with years of service even though productivity remains constant. Since workers receive compensation in excess of *P(H)* in later working years, the contract must terminate at some point. This could be the normal retirement age for the pension plan or the age of mandatory retirement. At this termination point, the present value of lifetime compensation must equal the present value of lifetime productivity.

Workers accept the contract if the utility from the higher present value of earnings based on the higher effort exceeds the disutility from providing higher rather than lower effort. For their part, firms do not arbitrarily renege on the contract because they wish to continue to make such contracts with younger workers. If a firm underpaid young workers and then did not honor the implied terms of the contract, future cohorts of new workers would not accept the contract offer. Thus, contracting models offer another explanation for why earnings increase with labor market experience. These contracts impose a penalty on workers who leave before the end of the contract. The penalty reduces mobility and increases productivity. It must be remembered, however, that cash earnings are not the only form of compensation in the employment relationship.

Pension Contracts. Returns to firm-specific human capital and rewards for higher levels of effort may be paid in the form of pension benefits from defined benefit plans. Therefore defined benefit pensions can be an important component of employment agreements between workers and firms. Workers agree to exchange labor for promises of future income in the form of pension benefits at retirement as well as for current cash earnings. The value of those future pension benefits depends upon the implied nature of the labor contract, the probability of the worker's survival, and government regulations. As mentioned earlier, defined contribution plans offer current compensation and therefore cannot be used to alter worker behavior.

Two methods of evaluating pension compensation and pension wealth have been proposed: the legal method and the projected-earnings method. Both assume that during their service with firms, workers pay for their pensions in the form of forgone earnings. The amount forgone in each period is the change in expected pension wealth due to continued employment,[4] which we call pension compensation. The methods differ in their assumptions about the value of benefits based on work to date. The legal method assumes that each period workers pay for the benefits to which they are legally entitled according to some formula based on current earnings and pension characteristics.[5] The projected-earnings method assumes that workers have implicitly contracted to be employed with the same firm until retirement and therefore are willing to pay in each period for the benefits they expect to receive at retirement.[6]

If cash earnings plus pension compensation are assumed to equal productivity in each period, the two methods yield different predictions about the slope of the earnings profile and turnover probabilities. The differences between these two models of pension evaluation are significant. If workers pay for only their legal pension, defined benefit pensions are explicit contracts. Workers pay only for the benefit they will receive when they leave the firm and there is no pension penalty. If this is true, defined benefit plans are not much different from defined contribution plans. If workers pay for a projected pension, however, defined benefit plans establish an implicit contract that imposes a pension penalty on mobile workers. Turnover therefore declines and productivity and worker compensation rise. The question is, which of these methods best captures the nature of the defined benefit pension contract?

Legal method. The basic premise of the legal method is the worker and firm behave as if the labor contract were valid for a single period. Of course, the contract may be renewed, but they act as if the contract will be terminated at the end of each period. Therefore, the worker is willing to pay in the form of forgone cash earnings only for those pension benefits that the firm is legally required to pay should the worker leave the firm at the end of the contract period.[7]

Suppose that a worker is covered by an earnings-based benefit formula. If the worker is fully vested, the benefit to which he is legally entitled if he leaves his current job is equal to the benefit based on the plan formula. The legal method assesses pension wealth from this benefit, given the earnings to date and current years of service. The worker's pension wealth is the expected value of a life annuity of B dollars per year beginning at the age of retirement discounted back to the current age of the worker. Pension compensation is the change in pension wealth attributable to an additional year of work. Before the plan retirement age, pension wealth and pension compensation increase with additional years of credited service, and with the growth of earnings. After the worker becomes eligible to begin receiving benefits, pension compensation will drop sharply because the worker must give up current benefits to continue working.[8]

Even if total compensation (earnings plus pension compensation) grows at the same rate as productivity, earnings will grow more slowly than productivity. This happens because the proportion of total compensation that goes to pension compensation increases rapidly as the worker ages.[9] Before the normal retirement age, pension compensation increases with age more rapidly than earnings or productivity. After the normal retirement age, pension compensation drops sharply and may become negative. If employment continues after the normal retirement age, earnings must increase sharply and exceed productivity in order for workers to continue to earn their marginal product.[10] If earnings do not increase, the worker receives a sharp reduction in total compensation and therefore has an economic incentive to retire.

Projected-earnings method. The basic premise of the projected-earnings method is that pensions are part of an implicit employment contract.[11] Each period the worker pays for a pension that he will receive if he remains with the firm and fulfills the contract. This can be called the stay pension. Its value exceeds the pension he will receive if he leaves the firm, which can be called the leave pension. If the worker thinks that the probability of quitting or of being laid off is very low, then he may be willing to exchange current earnings for the prospect of receiving the larger stay pension. It is assumed that the implicit contract ends at the normal retirement age, and that if the worker remains on the job after this age he will be hired on a one-year

37

explicit contract. In many plans, the benefit received at retirement is based on final earnings prior to retirement. The projected earnings method assumes that because the worker anticipates a full career with this firm, pension compensation is based on benefits expected at retirement. This expected benefit is a function of expected final earnings rather than of current earnings.

In this model, pension wealth increases only with the additional years of service, whereas in the legal model it increases with earnings and additional years of service. When years of service are low, according to the projected-earnings calculation, pension compensation is larger than actual legal pension compensation for which the firm is liable if the worker quits. Later in the person's work life, the legal pension compensation will exceed pension compensation based on projected earnings.

In contrast to the legal method, this method assumes that the worker pays more for pension coverage early in life and less in the final working years. Because earnings plus employee pension compensation are assumed to equal productivity in each period, earnings will grow more rapidly with the projected-earnings method. When the nominal wage grows at the same rate as the nominal interest, earnings will grow at the same rate as productivity and the worker will pay a constant proportion of his compensation or productivity in the form of forgone earnings each period. The projected earnings method also predicts a wage increase in the event of continued employment after the specified normal retirement age, because after the implicit contract ends, the wage must be equated to productivity in each period.

In this model, the worker is posting a bond in each pay period of his early working years. The value of the annual bond payment is the difference between the projected pension compensation and the legal pension compensation for that year. At any point in time, the accumulated value of these differences is equal to the projected pension wealth of the employee, less his legal pension wealth. This value is the pension loss incurred from leaving the job before retirement. As this value grows, the costs of quitting or being fired rise. The absolute magnitude of the accumulated bond peaks sometime before the end of the contract. The bond, or the loss from leaving, then declines and reaches zero at the normal age of retirement, when the implied labor contract has been completed.[12]

In the projected-earnings model, earnings plus projected pension compensation are assumed to equal worker productivity in every period. The projected pension benefit or stay pension payment exceeds the legal or leave pension benefit throughout the worker's career. As a result, the worker is underpaid relative to the legal compensation he would receive were he to quit or be fired. However, in the final years before the normal retirement age, the projected pension compensation is less than legal compensation, and the worker is overpaid relative to his productivity.

The total legal compensation and earnings profiles can be tilted further by relaxing the assumption that earnings plus pension compensation equal productivity in each period. In this case, the exact relationship between earnings and productivity will depend on the package of earnings and deferred compensation negotiated by the worker and firm. Thus, defined benefit plans can be used to encourage workers to modify their quitting behavior, the level of effort on the job, and the age of retirement. These contracts can enhance productivity and reduce costs for the firm while increasing lifetime compensation for the worker. The prospect of mutual gains through the pension contract is one of the principal advantages of defined benefit plans over defined contribution plans.

Incentive Effects of Pension Contracts

When employment agreements include pensions, the total compensation (or the returns to labor) is composed of pension accruals as well as cash earnings. Therefore, throughout their work lives with firms, workers will be motivated by the total returns to their labor. Although total compensation will depend on the specific provisions of each pension plan and the mix of cash earnings and deferred compensation negotiated by workers and firms, only earnings profiles and pension characteristics are ever observed. Projected and legal pension compensation must be inferred from the two.

The incentive effects of pensions are best summarized by their implied age-earnings and age-total compensation profiles. To illustrate these effects, we use a numerical model based on the lifetime pattern of earnings and pension compensation for a typical clerical worker in a small firm in the retail trade industry and for a typical production worker in a large manufacturing firm. Since similar results have been obtained for other categories of workers, these two examples suffice. In this model, total legal compensation consists of cash earnings plus legal pension compensation. Legal pension compensation varies with the parameters of the pension plan. The worker pays for the pension each year through a reduction in earnings such that earnings plus pension compensation equal the worker's marginal product. Earnings profiles and total compensation profiles are simulated using both the legal method and the projected-earnings method of evaluating pension wealth.[13]

The model assumes that each worker is hired by the firm at age

39

twenty-five. The total compensation rises by 2 percent per year in real terms. Throughout this analysis, total compensation is assumed to equal the value of the worker's productivity to the firm. Individuals are assumed to face the age-specific unisex mortality rates that existed in the United States in 1982.[14] Future dollars are discounted by a 2 percent real interest rate plus a 4 percent per year inflation rate. Nominal values of total compensation and wages are fully indexed to the inflation rate, and postretirement increases in pension benefits are 2 percent per year.

The clerical worker in our example is covered by a terminal-earnings formula based on the final five years of earnings (see table 3–5). The plan generosity parameter is 1.2 percent per year of service, and the age of eligibility for normal retirement benefits is sixty-three. Table 4–1 shows the life cycle pattern of earnings and total compensation for this worker at various ages using the legal method of assessing pension wealth. The initial total compensation for this worker is assumed to be $13,500. Therefore, this individual's average earnings from age twenty-five to age thirty-four are consistent with the average earnings of retail trade clerical workers in the same age bracket in the 1983 Current Population Survey (CPS). Also shown are legal pension compensation, pension wealth, and the percentage of total compensation allocated to pension compensation. If the legal method accurately reflects the workings of the labor contract, the value of pension compensation is equivalent to the increase in earnings that another employer without a pension would have to offer in order to provide the worker with the same total compensation that his current job provides. The percentage increase that would be required is shown in the last column of table 4–1. Thus, in the first year of employment, this worker receives $13,469 in earnings and $31 in legal pension compensation, or 0.2 percent of earnings. A worker would be indifferent if asked to choose between this compensation schedule and that of a firm offering $13,500 in cash earnings.

The pension produces several important effects. First, pension compensation increases more rapidly with age and tenure than do cash earnings until the normal retirement age. Consequently, the earnings profile is flatter than the total compensation profile. In our example, total compensation rises with productivity an average of 6 percent a year, while earnings increase an average of 5.4 percent a year. Pension compensation rises steadily as a percentage of earnings, peaking at 22.4 percent at age sixty-two (the year before normal retirement).

The second effect occurs at the normal retirement age, when

pension compensation declines abruptly because of the forgone bene-fit. In our example, earnings must increase 24.9 percent before total compensation will equal productivity in the year after the normal retirement age. If earnings do not rise, the worker has a strong incentive to retire.

In a labor contract that has evaluated benefits using the legal method, the worker has paid for only those future benefits that will be received, even if the worker quits before normal retirement. There-fore, there is no loss in pension wealth associated with quitting. However, the worker does forgo the opportunity to accumulate addi-tional benefits in that plan. As a result, before moving to an employer with no pension plan, he would want a wage increase equal to the percentage of total compensation going to pensions. In our example, the percentage rises from 1.7 percent at age thirty to 22.4 percent at age sixty-two, just before retirement. Since pension benefits rise with tenure and age, the worker who contemplates moving to a new firm

TABLE 4–1

LIFETIME COMPENSATION PROFILES (LEGAL METHOD):
HYPOTHETICAL CLERICAL WORKER IN A SMALL RETAIL TRADE FIRM
(dollars)

Age	Tenure	Earnings	Pension Compensation	Total Compensation	Pension Wealth	Pension Compensation as a Percentage of Earnings
25	0	13,469	31	13,500	0	0.2
30	5	17,819	316	18,134	1,172	1.7
35	10	23,666	693	24,360	4,222	2.8
40	15	31,269	1,453	32,722	11,372	4.4
45	20	41,007	2,948	43,955	27,179	6.7
50	25	53,223	5,821	59,043	60,871	9.9
55	30	68,109	11,203	79,312	131,011	14.1
60	35	85,537	21,002	106,539	274,750	19.7
62	37	93,090	26,798	119,887	367,744	22.4
63	38	116,291	10,886	127,177	425,168	8.6
64	39	124,092	10,817	134,909	459,210	8.0
65	40	132,536	10,575	143,111	495,670	7.4
70	45	200,000	−7,761	192,239	696,896	−4.0

SOURCE: Pension provisions shown in table 3–5 and worker characteristics from May Supplement, 1983 Current Population Survey.

TABLE 4–2

LIFETIME COMPENSATION PROFILES (PROJECTED-EARNINGS METHOD):
HYPOTHETICAL CLERICAL WORKER IN A SMALL RETAIL TRADE FIRM
(dollars)

Age	Tenure	Earnings	Projected Pension Compensation	Legal Pension Compensation	Pension Loss	Pension Loss as a Percentage of Earnings
25	0	12,384	1,116	29	0.0	0.0
30	5	16,627	1,508	297	6,448.1	38.8
35	10	22,321	2,039	660	16,429.2	73.6
40	15	29,960	2,761	1,418	30,629.9	102.2
45	20	40,197	3,757	2,984	48,870.7	121.6
50	25	53,889	5,154	6,212	68,424.8	127.0
55	30	72,149	7,163	12,886	79,844.1	110.7
60	35	96,402	10,137	26,825	56,509.7	58.6
62	37	108,159	11,728	36,065	24,336.6	22.5
63	38	121,909	5,268	5,268	0.0	0.0
64	39	130,496	4,413	4,413	0.0	0.0
65	40	139,787	3,324	3,324	0.0	0.0
70	45	204,997	−12,758	−12,758	0.0	0.0

SOURCE: Pension provisions shown in table 3–5 and worker characteristics
from May supplement, 1983 Current Population Survey.

where the pension plan is identical to that offered by his current
employer would also want an increase in cash earnings to keep his
total compensation equal to that received on the current job.

Note that if the worker has the same value to all employers, other
firms should be willing to offer higher cash earnings because they will
be required to provide less in the form of pension compensation.
Thus, if workers are paying for a legal pension under a defined
benefit plan, no employment contract is implied and pension compensation will be similar to cash compensation. At the end of each
period the worker is paid the value of his productivity in cash and
legally payable pension benefits. At any age the worker can move to
another firm that will pay him total compensation equal to productivity. There is no pension loss from such a move.

The compensation and earnings profiles for the clerical worker
derived using the projected-earnings method are shown in table 4–2.
This table also shows earnings and pension compensation at various
age-tenure combinations. Pension compensation and pension wealth

are based on the benefit if the worker remains with the firm until retirement. The pension loss to be expected from leaving is the difference between the wealth value of the stay pension (which the worker is assumed to have paid for in the form of reduced earnings) and the value of the worker's legal pension (which the firm will pay to terminated workers).

In this case, the worker pays for a benefit based on final earnings; therefore, the proportion of earnings forgone each year rises only slightly with age. The earnings profile is steeper than the profile implied by the legal method. Earnings increase at the same rate as productivity plus inflation, or an average of 6 percent per year. Pension compensation also declines at the age of normal retirement. The implied increase in earnings at eligibility is 12.7 percent.

If this model correctly captures the essence of the labor contract, quitting produces a real loss in pension wealth because a larger proportion of forgone earnings has gone to pension compensation in the early working years. Competing employers must offer more in total compensation than is currently being received on the present job to entice the worker to quit voluntarily. The loss in pension benefits associated with quitting and the loss as a percentage of earnings are shown in the last two columns of table 4–2. The loss rises rapidly during the first twenty years of work life, declines through the later working years, and finally reaches zero at the normal retirement age. The loss from quitting actually exceeds cash earnings from the time the worker has fifteen years of experience to the last years before reaching normal retirement age.

Our representative plan for production workers in large manufacturing firms is based on dollars per year of service, with full eligibility after thirty years of service. Simulated profiles for this type of plan are shown in tables 4–3 and 4–4. Total compensation at age twenty-five is $15,000 and benefits accrue at a rate of $190.08 for each year of service. It is assumed that the dollar amount per year of service increases 6 percent a year to reflect inflation and productivity growth. If the legal method is used to calculate pension payments, a larger proportion of total compensation goes to pension compensation than was true for the clerical worker (table 4–3). At age twenty-five the worker receives cash earnings of $14,572 along with a pension compensation of $428. At age fifty, pension compensation is equal to almost half of cash earnings. As a result, the earnings profile is much flatter than that for the clerical worker. Pension compensation drops 73 percent at the age of normal retirement. Earnings increase an average of 4.1 percent a year compared with the 6.0 percent increase in total compensation.

TABLE 4–3

LIFETIME COMPENSATION PROFILES (LEGAL METHOD):
HYPOTHETICAL PRODUCTION WORKER IN
A LARGE MANUFACTURING FIRM
(dollars)

Age	Tenure	Earnings	Pension Compensation	Total Compensation	Pension Wealth	Pension Compensation as a Percentage of Earnings
25	0	14,572	428	15,000	0	2.9
30	5	19,157	993	20,149	3,649	5.2
35	10	24,874	2,192	27,066	13,206	8.8
40	15	31,665	4,692	36,357	35,910	14.8
45	20	38,987	9,851	48,838	87,180	25.3
50	25	45,118	20,486	65,604	200,057	45.4
54	29	46,314	36,760	83,074	380,729	79.4
55	30	78,315	9,809	88,124	446,441	12.5
56	31	84,393	9,089	93,482	477,348	10.8
60	35	114,316	4,061	118,376	611,333	3.6
65	40	168,501	− 9,488	159,013	794,406	− 5.6
70	45	250,298	− 36,699	213,599	969,865	− 14.7

SOURCE: Pension provisions shown in table 3–5 and worker characteristics from May supplement, 1983 Current Population Survey.

The increase in earnings required to offset the decline in pension compensation after the normal retirement age is 69.1 percent.

The projected-earnings profiles shown in table 4–4 also imply that a greater proportion of cash earnings are forgone under this plan. Because the production worker is eligible for full benefits after thirty years of service, pension compensation is much higher than it is for the clerical worker, who is not eligible until after thirty-eight years of service. The decline in pension compensation at the normal retirement age is only 13.2 percent compared with the 69.1 percent implied by the legal method. The loss associated with quitting rises for the first twenty-three years of service and exceeds earnings in most years. At age fifty, the loss associated with quitting before retirement represents 123 percent of annual earnings.

The pension cost of changing jobs is a function of various defined benefit plan provisions. Firms with large hiring and training costs can be expected to impose large pension penalties to restrict the mobility of workers. Even before they accept employment with such firms, workers know that quitting carries a pension penalty. Firms can also use defined benefit plans to encourage earlier or later retirements by altering pension compensation for older workers.

If workers pay for a projected pension, all of these incentives can be imposed by firms using defined benefit plans. Similar incentives are not present in defined contribution plans because few conditions are placed on the value of the pension. Therefore, companies can use defined benefit plans in their compensation package to achieve various personnel objectives. Because these pension contracts lower firm costs, firms may be willing to pay part of the costs of defined benefit plans.

Evaluating Pension Compensation and Pension Wealth

Which of the two methods just discussed will produce a true measure of the value of a pension? Which best reflects how worker compensation operates? To examine these questions, we compare the predictions each method makes concerning earnings, quits, and retirement

TABLE 4–4

LIFETIME COMPENSATION PROFILES (PROJECTED-EARNINGS METHOD):
HYPOTHETICAL PRODUCTION WORKER IN
A LARGE MANUFACTURING FIRM
(dollars)

Age	Tenure	Earnings	Projected Pension Compensation	Legal Pension Compensation	Pension Loss	Pension Loss as a Percentage of Earnings
25	0	12,682	2,318	428	0.0	0.0
30	5	17,017	3,132	993	12,011.8	70.6
35	10	22,831	4,235	2,192	29,147.7	127.7
40	15	30,620	5,737	4,692	50,149.9	163.8
45	20	41,032	7,806	9,851	68,946.1	168.0
50	25	54,895	10,709	20,486	67,664.4	123.3
54	29	69,157	13,916	36,760	22,843.7	33.0
55	30	78,315	9,809	9,809	0.0	0.0
56	31	84,393	9,089	9,089	0.0	0.0
60	35	114,316	4,061	4,061	0.0	0.0
65	40	168,501	−9,488	−9,488	0.0	0.0
70	45	250,298	−36,699	−36,699	0.0	0.0

SOURCE: Pension provisions shown in table 3–5 and worker characteristics from May supplement, 1983 Current Population Survey.

and the findings of empirical studies that have tested for pension effects.

Pensions and Earnings Profiles. According to the legal method, workers pay for vested pension benefits in each pay period. If that is the case, then the value of annual earnings depends on annual pension compensation. Legal pension compensation varies substantially from year to year and exhibits large jumps at vesting, the age for early retirement, and the age for normal retirement. Thus, if this method correctly captures the nature of the pension contract, earnings should fall when the worker becomes vested or passes the age of eligibility for early retirement.

Ignoring these jumps at particular points in the work life, the legal method predicts that earnings will grow at a slower rate than worker productivity. The implication is that the earnings of pension-covered workers will grow at a slower pace than the earnings of workers not covered by pensions. In contrast, the projected-earnings method assumes that workers look forward to retirement with the firm and base the value of their pensions on final earnings with the company. They pay for this stay pension throughout their work lives. Therefore, this model predicts a smoother earnings growth for pension participants, and the slope of the age-earnings profile will not differ greatly from that of workers who are not covered by a pension.

Only a few studies have attempted to estimate the effect of pensions on the earnings of workers. These studies have found that earnings do not rise more slowly for pension participants.[15] Nor do they detect jumps in earnings associated with vesting and qualifying for early retirement. Consequently, they support the notion that workers pay for a projected benefit, not a legal one.

Pensions and Mobility. If workers pay for a pension in the way that the legal method suggests, they pay only for the pension they will receive if they leave the firm. As a result, there is no pension loss associated with job termination and pensions should not influence labor market turnover. If workers pay for a projected pension on the basis of continued employment with the firm, the value of this stay pension will exceed the value of the leave pension determined by the legal method. Thus, these workers face a capital loss in their pension wealth if they leave the firm before retirement.

Relatively few empirical studies have attempted to estimate the effect of pension coverage and pension characteristics on mobility. Because of data limitations, most of these studies have been unable to determine if the pension under consideration is a defined contribution or a defined benefit plan. Throughout this book we have argued that defined benefit plans tend to reduce the frequency of job changes, whereas defined contribution plans do not alter mobility plans. The only attempt that has been made to measure the effect of specific provisions on mobility[16] did not derive a pension loss from job changes. Nonetheless, the results of that analysis can be used to speculate on the effects of pensions on labor mobility. The study was based on two samples of persons covered by 133 pension plans. The objective was to determine whether any plan characteristics correlated with the decision to leave an employer in 1979. Higher exit rates occurred in plans with strict vesting requirements and eligibility for early retirement before age sixty. The impact of other factors such as benefit amount and contributory status varied across the two samples.

Another study has provided some information on the effect of pension coverage on quits and job changes in a longitudinal sample from the 1973 and 1977 Quality of Employment Survey conducted by the University of Michigan Survey Research Center.[17] Males were found to be 10 percent less likely to quit if they were covered by a pension plan. Pension coverage had a smaller and statistically insignificant effect on quits among females. Job changes (including quits and layoffs) were much less likely to occur among both males and females covered by pensions. The finding that pension coverage reduces job turnover has also been reported elsewhere.[18]

In addition, several studies have found a strong relationship between pension coverage and mobility or job tenure. Pension coverage may indeed be an important determinant of job tenure, exceeding the effect of unionization,[19] but firm size can also have a strong effect.[20]

The relationship between actual pension costs and turnover can be studied by deriving "stay pension wealth" (using the projected-earnings method) and "leave pension wealth" (using the legal method).[21] The difference in these values is the capital loss associated with a job change. Workers facing a larger capital loss should be less likely to quit. When this suggestion was tested on 1979 CPS data, pension loss had an insignificant effect on job mobility, whereas coverage had a strong effect. In the federal civil service, however, the high capital loss facing workers who leave helps to explain the relatively low quit rates among government employees.[22]

It has also been suggested that the mechanisms through which pension coverage reduces labor mobility are the large capital losses in pension wealth associated with leaving a job and the ability of firms with pensions to attract more stable workers.[23] Vesting status and the

47

greater compensation associated with pension coverage apparently have little impact on mobility. These results are obtained from mobility equations estimated separately by pension coverage status and adjusting for selection bias with respect to pension coverage. When turnover probabilities are examined across workers covered by pensions, the capital loss is associated with lower turnover rates, whereas vesting and compensation levels have relatively little impact.[24]

Pensions and Retirement. All defined benefit plans set a normal retirement age at which workers can retire with full retirement benefits. Under current law, firms cannot demand that workers retire at this or any specific age, nor can the cash earnings of older workers be arbitrarily lowered. If workers wish to continue working, they must continue to receive pension accruals based on higher earnings and additional years of service. Despite these restrictions, firms can still use defined benefit plans to provide significant retirement incentives, because pension compensation drops substantially for individuals who remain on the job past the normal retirement age.

Pension compensation declines even with full wage and service accruals because the worker forgoes current pension benefits to remain on the job, and future benefits are usually not adjusted upward to account for the reduced number of remaining years of life. This is the case whether pensions are evaluated using the legal or the projected method. Since both methods yield similar predictions concerning the impact of defined benefit coverage on retirement behavior, we need to find another means of determining which is the most appropriate method of evaluating defined benefit pension wealth.

Unless defined contribution plans cease contributions at the normal retirement age (which is now illegal), these plans do not alter the gain from working as the individual ages. Thus, we expect workers covered by defined contribution plans to have retirement patterns more like those of persons not covered by any pension than those of participants in defined benefit plans. Unfortunately, this hypothesis has not yet been fully tested.

Over the past two decades, many studies have examined retirement decisions and the role of employer pensions. The earliest research included only a pension coverage variable or an estimated value of pension benefits to measure the effect of pensions on retirement.[25] More recent studies have attempted to model the pension contract and to determine how the pension alters the budget constraint facing older workers.[26] These studies have introduced the concept of pension compensation into the retirement function. Virtually all studies have found that pension coverage lowers the retirement age and that a decline in pension compensation encourages earlier retirement.

Which Method Should Be Used? Several conclusions can be drawn from past research on pension issues. First, workers pay for a projected, or stay, pension. Thus, in determining pension wealth and the pension cost of changing jobs, the correct method of evaluating the pension is the projected-earnings method. Second, defined benefit plans are used as part of productivity-enhancing employment contracts. Third, legally vested pension wealth is also a valid concept, since it is used to determine the value of the leave pension. Thus the legal method should be used to determine the realized pension wealth for mobile workers. The critical point here is that a distinction must be made between the pension workers pay for and the pension they actually receive if they leave the firm before the normal retirement age. Without this distinction, it is impossible to assess correctly the influence of defined benefit plans on worker behavior.

5
Pension Wealth and Job Mobility

When used in conjunction with a firm's other personnel policies, defined benefit plans can modify workers' behavior. As already pointed out, workers who face the prospect of less pension wealth if they change jobs are more likely to remain with their employers. Firms with defined benefit plans promise in effect to retain the worker until retirement on the condition that the worker satisfies certain work and productivity requirements. By lowering quit and layoff rates and thereby increasing job tenure and reducing the firm's turnover costs, such implicit employment contracts can make all parties, workers and firms, better off. With longer expected tenure, workers and firms are more willing to invest in firm-specific skills. Thus, lifetime productivity and lifetime earnings will rise.

Defined contribution plans, on the other hand, provide current compensation for current work and are not part of contingent agreements to modify worker behavior. In defined contribution plans, the worker has a direct claim on the value of the funds in his pension account. Once vested, if he quits, is laid off, or fired, the worker can take these funds with him and not lose any pension wealth because defined contribution plans are fullfunded and the worker owns the pension account. These plans are used to increase the net after-tax income of workers in each period. To the extent that they increase total compensation, defined contribution plans help firms attract and maintain employees in the same manner as higher cash wages.

The wealth value of a worker's pension at retirement in a defined benefit plan is determined by, among other factors, the generosity of the benefit formula, the worker's lifetime pattern of earnings, and the frequency of job changes throughout the work life. Pension wealth also is influenced by employer practices and government regulations that fix minimum standards for the vesting of pension benefits, portability of service credits, and lump-sum cash distributions.

Pension Wealth and Job Change in Defined Benefit Plans

Numerical analyses can be used to compare realized pension wealth at retirement for workers who change jobs and the pension wealth for those who remain with a single employer.

50

If there were no vesting or portability, a worker leaving an employer would not be entitled to any pension benefits at retirement from that job. Vesting of benefits ensures that the worker will receive a benefit based on his work history at the firm. Even with vesting, the mobile worker will have lower pension wealth unless service credits are portable. The magnitude of the loss in the absence of portability is determined by the plan formula. With final-pay formulas, the pension loss is large, whereas career-average formulas sharply reduce the loss. Thus, the magnitude of the loss is determined by the length of the period used to determine the average salary in the benefit formula. Lump-sum distributions might limit this loss, but almost certainly would not eliminate it.

Vesting of Pension Benefits. Vesting of pension benefits accrued to date means that a worker who quits his job retains the legal right to a future pension benefit. This benefit is based on the current benefit formula in effect at the time of termination and the worker's years of service and/or earnings with that firm. Before ERISA was enacted in 1974, there were no government regulations concerning vesting and many firms set vesting in defined benefit plans to occur at retirement. ERISA established three alternative minimum standards for pension plans; however, most plans are based on the ten-year, 100 percent vesting standard. This meant that workers who left their employers before serving ten years received no benefits, but after ten years could leave with their legal benefits based on earnings to date fully vested.

In 1986, Congress lowered vesting standards, effective in 1989, to five-year, 100 percent vesting, or graded vesting, beginning with 20 percent vesting after three years. Most plans will probably switch to the five-year, 100 percent vesting standards because it simplifies plan administration. With the reduction in the vesting requirements, most workers covered by a pension will remain with their companies long enough to qualify for a vested benefit. Although the service requirements for vesting may be lowered in the future, any further reduction will have only a minor impact on pension wealth at retirement because benefits are relatively low if one has put in only a few years of work. Therefore, even the frequent job changer would receive only minor increases in pension wealth at retirement from further reductions in vesting standards.

The current standards accord considerable certainty in terms of the future receipt of pension benefits because most workers eventually find a job in which they attain considerable job tenure. This is especially true among workers covered by a pension.[1] Thus, the currently mandated low vesting standard will ensure that most pension participants receive a benefit based on current employment history and the existing benefit formula. However, these benefits typically are frozen in nominal terms and thus do not rise with inflation, growth in real wages, or plan improvements.

Portability of Service Credits. When a worker with a vested benefit leaves a job covered by a single-employer, defined benefit plan, pension benefits are fixed at a level specified by the prevailing benefit formula and are deferred until retirement. Generally, workers do not have the option of transferring their accrued service credits to their new employers because they do not own the plan assets and therefore have no specific pension account. Rather the difference between the worker's stay pension and the leave pension is forfeited to the firm. These funds were allowed to accumulate on the condition that the worker would honor the implicit contract. Since he has violated the contract, the funds revert to the employer.

As a result of terminal-earnings benefit formulas and this lack of portability of service credits, job changers with similar earnings histories will have lower benefits at retirement than persons who spend their entire work lives with a single firm. This is true even if the mobile worker is fully vested and entitled to receive a pension from each of his jobs. While vesting is important, it does not fully account for pension loss from job changes. The primary reason for lower pension benefits is that the pensions from earlier jobs for the mobile worker are based on earnings at various points during the work life, whereas benefits for the worker who sticks with a single job tend to be determined by final earnings.

If service credits were transferred from one firm to another with the worker, his final benefit from his employer would be unaffected by job changes. Given the widespread use of terminal-benefit for-mulas, the lack of portability of service credits is the main reason why participants in defined benefit plans lose pension wealth when they change jobs. The magnitude of the pension loss is governed by the benefit formula and economic conditions. For example, workers covered by career-average formulas will experience much smaller pension losses when they change jobs. Thus, a switch to greater use of career-average formulas would also reduce the pension loss associated with job changes.

Multi-employer, defined benefit plans allow workers to move across firms participating in the plan while retaining all service credits. Workers in multi-employer plans have full portability of service credits as long as they move only among the firms in the pension plan. If workers move to an employer outside the plan, they will receive their vested benefit at retirement, but rarely will their service credits be portable outside the multi-employer group. Thus, job changes to employers outside the participating firms will result in the same type of pension loss as that suffered by workers who leave single-employer defined benefit plans.

The extent to which the lack of portability affects pension wealth depends on whether a worker is likely to leave a particular employer. Defined benefit plans have been adopted by many large companies and cover thousands of employees and many different types of jobs in many different locations. Participants in these plans can change jobs and move across states with the same employer and retain all pension rights. The lower turnover and greater job security in these firms helps explain why workers are more willing to accept labor market risks associated with defined benefit plans if they work for a large company.

Lump-sum Distributions. Pension wealth may also be lost if the worker does not have access to pension funds at the time of job termination. The present value of future pension benefits (based on the person's work history at the time of termination) could be calculated and made available to the departing employee. For example, ERISA allowed firms to involuntarily cash out workers who had a present value of pension wealth less than $1,750; the 1984 Retirement Equity Act raised this value to $3,500. The lifetime wealth of workers will be boosted under a policy of lump-sum distributions if they are able to invest these funds at a rate that exceeds the interest rate used to determine the wealth value of the cash disbursement. In order to achieve higher expected returns, investors must assume increased risks. On average, the right to receive a lump-sum distribution of vested benefits will not increase the lifetime pension wealth of job changers. Lump-sum distributions are now widely available to participants of defined contribution plans.[2] In contrast, participants in defined benefit plans are less likely to be able to request cash-outs of vested pension values.

Pension Wealth Profiles and Job Changes

Consider the pension cost of changing jobs for two hypothetical workers covered by the average defined benefit in the retail trade (see table 3–5). One of these workers is initially hired on a job at age twenty-five and works each year until the normal retirement age of the plan, which is age sixty-three. The other worker stays with the first employer for five years and then changes to a new employer. The second job lasts ten years and is followed by a third ten-year job. The

TABLE 5–1

EARNINGS AND PENSION PROFILES: SINGLE JOB

(dollars)

Age	Tenure	Earnings	Benefit[a]	Nominal Pension Wealth	Real Pension Wealth[b]
25	0	13,500	0	0	0
30	5	18,134	915	1,015	834
35	10	24,360	2,457	3,686	2,490
40	15	32,722	4,951	10,062	5,587
45	20	43,955	8,868	24,520	11,191
50	25	59,043	14,890	56,480	21,187
55	30	79,312	24,002	126,516	39,007
60	35	106,539	37,616	280,589	71,106
62	37	119,887	44,747	386,207	90,487
63	38	127,177	48,751	453,423	102,150

a. Benefit is the pension that the worker could receive at age sixty-three on the basis of work to date.
b. Real pension wealth is nominal pension wealth deflated back to age twenty-five dollars.
SOURCE: Clerical workers in small retail trade firms, U.S. Bureau of Labor Statistics, *Employee Benefits Survey of Medium and Large Firms, 1983.*

worker then takes a fourth job, which lasts for the final thirteen years of work.

Earnings are assumed to be unaffected by job changes, so that differences in the accumulation of pension wealth are attributable solely to the movement into and out of pension plans. It is further assumed that workers move among firms that have identical pension plans so as to isolate the effect on pension wealth of quitting. In reality, job changes almost always result in changes in earnings and participation in a new pension plan that is considerably different from the one on the previous job. If job changes are initiated by the worker, one would expect the firm bidding the worker away from his old job to compensate him for any loss in lifetime pension benefits by offering higher earnings and fringe benefits than the previous employer.

The worker's initial annual salary is set at $13,500 and nominal earnings are assumed to grow at 6 percent per year until retirement. This increase is based on an assumed growth in real earnings of 2 percent and annual inflation of 4.0 percent. For this analysis, the possibility of early retirement is ignored and pension wealth is calculated at an expected retirement age of sixty-three. The worker is assumed to be fully vested after one year of service and to be single or, equivalently, to have selected single-life annuity benefits.[3]

Pension Wealth from a Single Job. Annual earnings for various age and tenure are shown in table 5–1. These values reflect the annual compensation for working at the age-tenure levels shown in the first two columns. Since we are examining the effects of job changes on pension wealth, the benefit column indicates the retirement benefit the worker would receive at age sixty-three if he stopped working at the specified age. Legal pension wealth is based on this benefit, which is the legal or leave pension discussed in chapter 4.

As the worker ages and accumulates more job tenure, pension wealth grows rapidly. By age sixty-three, the worker has accumulated a nominal pension wealth of over $453,000. Adjusting this amount for thirty-eight years of inflation yields a pension wealth of just over $100,000 in age twenty-five dollars. Replacement rates (pension benefits as a proportion of final earnings) can be calculated by dividing the benefit at sixty-three by final earnings at age sixty-two. In this example, the worker has a replacement rate of 40.7 percent.

Job Changes without Cash-outs. The compensation and wealth patterns for a worker with four jobs during his career is illustrated in table 5–2.[4] Job changes do not affect annual earnings in these simulations and each firm is assumed to have the same pension plan. The table shows annual earnings at the age of each job change. The pension wealth shown at the specified ages is associated only with the current job. Thus, pension wealth is the expected value of the benefits the worker will receive if he terminates employment at the specified age. At age thirty, the worker has $1,015 in pension wealth from the work to date on his first job. If he remains on this job, his earnings will be $18,134 during his thirtieth year. However, he moves to a new employer, who also pays $18,134. Since he is not vested in this new job, he receives no pension compensation and has no pension wealth from this job. As pointed out earlier, the worker would not make such a move voluntarily because it implies a reduction in total compensation. However, workers who have been involuntarily separated from their pension-covered job may find it difficult to obtain comparable total compensation on a new job.

When the lifetime compensation of the worker with a single job (table 5–1) is compared with that of the job changer (table 5–2), several expected differences emerge. Pension wealth on the current job drops to zero every time the worker changes jobs. This decline occurs because pension wealth is based on the worker's vested pen-

TABLE 5–2
Earnings and Pension Profiles: Four Jobs
(dollars)

Age	Tenure	Earnings	Benefit[a]	Nominal Pension Wealth	Real Pension Wealth[b]
25	0	13,500	0	0	0
30	5	18,134	915	1,015	834
30	0	18,134	0	0	0
35	5	24,360	1,229	1,843	1,245
40	10	32,722	3,301	6,708	3,725
40	0	32,722	0	0	0
45	5	43,955	2,217	6,130	2,798
50	10	59,043	5,956	22,592	8,475
50	0	59,043	0	0	0
55	5	79,312	4,000	21,086	6,501
60	10	106,539	10,747	80,168	20,316
62	12	119,887	14,513	125,256	29,347
63	13	127,177	16,678	155,118	34,946
Total pension wealth at age 63				$249,723	$56,259

a. Benefit is the pension that the worker could receive at age sixty-three on the basis of work to date.
b. Real pension wealth is nominal pension wealth deflated back to age twenty-five dollars.
Source: Clerical workers in small retail trade firms, U.S. Bureau of Labor Statistics, *Employee Benefits Survey of Medium and Large Firms, 1983.*

sion benefit, which is affected by years of service, current earnings, vesting, and the lack of portability. Switching jobs, therefore, implies lower pension compensation at each age. Of course, this results in lower total pension wealth from all jobs. This is easily shown by adding the four pension benefits and comparing this total and the pension wealth shown in table 5–1. Total pension wealth for the job changer is $249,723, or only 55.1 percent of the wealth of the single-job worker.

In this example, if plan provisions are held constant, the decline in pension wealth associated with a job change is a reflection of the lack of portability of service credits across firms for a defined benefit plan with a final-average formula. The more frequent the job changes, the greater the lifetime loss of pension wealth resulting from the lack of portability. If new employers counted previous years of pension participation at other firms, pension wealth would be the same for both the job changer and the single-job worker.

The magnitude of the pension loss is determined by plan provisions and economic conditions. For example, workers covered by final-earnings plans whose nominal earnings increase rapidly will incur greater losses in real pension wealth with job changes. Therefore, increases in the rate of inflation will increase the loss in pension wealth of the job changers. This is easily shown by examining the difference between benefits based on nominal earnings at various points in the work life and benefits based on earnings at retirement. Increases in real earnings will have similar effects. However, the pension loss is reduced the more years that are included in the salary averaging period. In fact, the loss is eliminated through the use of a career-average benefit formula.

Tables 5–1 and 5–2 also show the effects of vesting on the accumulation of pension wealth. If, as in the pre-ERISA days, workers vested only at retirement, the job changer would have zero pension wealth from all jobs except his last job. In the example of clerical workers in small retail firms, vested benefits from earlier jobs account for one-third of the total pension wealth of the job changer. The ratio of the value of vested benefits from previous jobs to total pension wealth is inversely related to the length of the last job. Thus, for many job changers, vested benefits will represent a considerable proportion of pension wealth.

Whether the loss in pension wealth is a loss in total wealth depends on whether the job change was voluntary or involuntary. If the worker voluntarily quits to move to a new firm, the value of the new job is presumably sufficient to compensate the worker for the pension loss. In this case, the worker violates the employment contract by accepting a new job and is penalized on the basis of the previously agreed pension contract. Including the loss in pension wealth, the worker is made better off by the change. The pension penalty helps to compensate the firm for its lost investment. In this scenario, the pension loss can be viewed as indicating the minimum increase in total compensation necessary to entice a worker to leave the current job.

The pension loss is a real loss in lifetime wealth if the worker is involuntarily terminated by the firm. In this case, the worker suffers the loss in pension wealth without receiving any compensation. The losses described in this chapter pertain only to pension loss and do not reflect any potential gains in the form of higher compensation associated with voluntary job changes. Thus, they are best viewed as (1) pension penalties that reduce the probability that a worker will voluntarily change jobs and (2) the actual pension loss to workers who are involuntarily terminated.

Job Changes with Cash-outs. Thus far, job changes have been shown to reduce pension wealth substantially at retirement, even when all retirement benefits were fully vested and the worker received a pension from each job. A policy of cashing out pension wealth at the time of job termination is easily implemented. Would mobile workers benefit from new regulations requiring firms to provide lump-sum distributions? The possible effect of such regulations can be examined in the framework of our model for the average defined benefit plan. The cash value of any disbursement would be equal to the pension wealth at the time of the job termination. Recall that pension wealth in this model is the expected value of a life annuity beginning at age sixty-three discounted back to the current age by both an interest rate factor and a survivorship factor. Assume that new regulations require that prevailing market interest rates be used to calculate pension wealth while on the job as well as to determine the cash-out value of pension wealth upon job termination. The interest rate is assumed to be 6 percent in the simulations below.

Table 5–3 shows the total pension wealth of the job changer assuming that he accepts lump-sum distributions when he leaves his first three jobs. Since the worker is assumed to retire from the fourth job, he receives the pension from this job in the form of a retirement annuity. Suppose that he takes the cash from the distributions and invests it. Table 5–3 shows the value of these investments at age sixty-three under four alternative rates of return. These rates of return show the effect of the individual being able to do slightly better than the market interest rate (7 percent return), slightly worse than the market (5 percent return), much better than the market rate (11 percent return), and much worse than the market (1 percent return).

The alternative investments yield expected results. For example, pension wealth with cash-outs ranges from a low of $190,672 for rate of return of 1 percent to a high of $348,583 when the rate of return is 11 percent. These values can be compared to pension wealth of $249,723 without cash-outs. In this example, the worst outcome from personal investments is pension wealth that is 55 percent of the value of the best investment performance and 76 percent of the no cash-out value.

In these examples, investors who are able to achieve rates of return that exceed the interest rate used to determine their lump-sum distributions are able to limit the pension loss from job changes. In general, investment strategies designed to achieve above-market returns entail a high degree of risk, thus increasing the likelihood of below-market returns. In summary, lump-sum disbursements offer the potential for reducing the pension penalty but only with a higher investment risk.

Pension Cost of Changing Jobs in the U.S. Economy

We now turn from hypothetical workers to actual workers covered by the Employee Benefits Survey (EBS) and the Current Population Survey of 1983 to construct the expected pension loss in various industries. The typical pension formulas used by employers in the EBS (see table 3–5) are assumed to represent the pensions covering workers in the 1983 CPS. Because the CPS contains no information on plan type, we assume that all the workers in each industry-occupation-size grouping are covered by the modal plan from the EBS. All of these plans are defined benefit plans; therefore, this assumption has the effect of assigning all pension participants to defined benefit plans.

Using personal data on length of service at their current jobs and earnings reported by the respondents, we calculate for each individual the pension wealth based on expected earnings at retirement (the projected earnings method) and the legal pension wealth of the

TABLE 5–3

PENSION WEALTH AT AGE SIXTY-THREE FOR A SINGLE JOB
AND FOR FOUR JOBS
(dollars)

Work History and Distribution Rules	Last Job		Cash from Lump-Sum Distributions	Total Pension Wealth	
	Benefit at Retirement	Pension Wealth		Nominal	Real[a]
Single job	48,751	453,423		453,423	102,150
Four jobs					
Without cash-outs	26,859[b]	249,723[b]		249,723	56,259
With cash-outs					
Rate of Return (%)					
1	16,678	155,118	35,554	190,672	42,956
5	16,678	155,118	68,281	223,400	50,326
7	16,678	155,118	95,705	250,824	56,507
11	16,678	155,118	193,464	348,583	78,531

a. All values are in age twenty-five dollars.
b. These values represent the sum of pensions from all four jobs in this example.
SOURCE: See tables 5–1 and 5–2.

worker. The difference between projected and legal pension wealth at a particular age is the pension cost of leaving a job. The prevailing interest rate in 1983 was 9 percent, which is the rate used to calculate pension wealth here. The pension loss is determined for all respondents in the CPS who are covered by a pension in their 1983 jobs.[5]

Table 5–4 presents the mean pension loss for all workers covered by a pension in the various age-industry categories. The dollar values show the loss in pension wealth incurred if the average worker in this category changed jobs. For example, workers aged thirty-five to fifty-four in manufacturing face a pension loss of $12,000 to $14,000 if they change jobs. This represents about half a year's earnings for these workers. Absolute and relative losses are much lower in the service sector.

Even within an industry, benefit formulas vary considerably across occupational groups. To allow for these differences, we determined the magnitude of pension loss by occupation within the various industries. Among professional workers, the dollar value of the loss is much higher in the manufacturing and financial sectors than in the service sector. In the manufacturing and financial industries, the loss for the average professional worker aged thirty-five to fifty-four is approximately $25,000. The loss as a proportion of a year's earnings is also higher for professional workers; it ranges from 60 to 75 percent of a year's salary for workers in the manufacturing and financial sectors.

As expected, the age pattern of the pension loss indicates that the cost of leaving is relatively low early in one's work life, when total pension wealth is low. The loss associated with job changes increases with continued work until around age fifty, when the loss peaks. The pension loss then declines until it reaches zero at the normal retirement age. This pattern is similar to the patterns shown in chapter 4 for the hypothetical workers. The average participant in a defined benefit plan between the ages of thirty-five and fifty-four must forfeit approximately half a year's earnings to change jobs. This cost is in addition to any other search and moving costs the individual incurs when switching employers.

One of the primary objectives of pension contracts is to reduce employee turnover. This leads to greater investment in human capital and reduces labor costs. However, if economic conditions decline, employers may want more of their workers to quit. Under adverse economic conditions, anticipated future wage increases do not materialize, and so more workers may desire to quit. In these circumstances, potential pension loss retards the labor force adjustment that would have occurred if compensation was based on an explicit employment contract.

TABLE 5–4

Pension Loss for Workers Covered by a Pension in 1983, by Age and Industry
(dollars)

Age	Mining	Construction	Manufacturing		Transportation, Communications, Utilities	Trade	Finance, Insurance, Real Estate	Services
			Durable	Nondurable				
25–34	11,034	3,403	6,048	5,891	11,501	5,249	6,358	4,029
	(.42)	(.13)	(.29)	(.30)	(.49)	(.26)	(.33)	(.21)
35–44	19,572	6,625	13,947	11,751	18,529	10,682	14,886	9,341
	(.65)	(.23)	(.54)	(.51)	(.72)	(.47)	(.60)	(.35)
45–54	13,490	7,869	13,112	11,852	10,630	12,215	19,828	10,744
	(.49)	(.28)	(.53)	(.59)	(.40)	(.54)	(.79)	(.44)
55–64	9,808	4,384	6,944	6,069	5,452	8,855	10,638	9,721
	(.25)	(.17)	(.33)	(.33)	(.21)	(.44)	(.50)	(.39)

NOTE: Values in parentheses indicate the sample mean of the pension loss divided by the sample mean of annual earnings.
SOURCE: Steven Allen, Robert Clark, and Ann McDermed, "The Pension Cost of Changing Jobs," *Research on Aging* (December 1988), p. 465.

Pension coverage rates vary by industry. A larger fraction of workers in manufacturing and mining are covered by pensions than in other industries. Between 1979 and 1983, employment in these industries declined; for example, employment in durable manufacturing declined by 3 percent. In contrast, low pension coverage rates are found in the trade, financial, and service sectors, which have been growing relatively rapidly. Employment in these sectors increased between 1979 and 1983. Therefore, the potential for pensions to reduce employee quits is greatest in the sectors of the economy that have been declining in total employment. This suggests that the labor force in these industries will tend to age more rapidly than the labor force at large. This follows from the reduced hiring of young workers, coupled with the low quit rates among older workers. In these sectors, the pension contract slows the adjustment to the decline in product demand.

Pension Loss and Public Policy

Participants in defined benefit plans accept an implicit employment contract that imposes a loss in pension wealth if they leave the firm before retirement. Our analysis in chapters 4 and 5 indicates that the magnitude of this loss is a function of the benefit formula, vesting and portability standards, and economic conditions. The existence of this pension penalty for changing jobs is the enforcement mechanism of the contract that reduces worker quits, increases tenure, raises investment in training, and thus increases productivity. Workers accept these contracts because participation brings the reward of higher lifetime compensation, provided they fulfill the specified terms.

Given the terms of the contract, workers who voluntarily leave their jobs should consider the pension penalty a cost of changing jobs. If after considering this cost they quit, they have concluded that a new job offer is sufficiently attractive to entice them away from the current employer, even though they must forfeit a portion of pension wealth. Within this framework, there seems little reason for the government to attempt to limit the pension cost of changing jobs.

The firm honors the implicit contract because it wants to maintain its labor market reputation and continue to offer productivity-enhancing contracts. The value of current and future contracts may decline with adverse economic conditions. When the demand for products declines, the demand for workers also drops. Firms may therefore attempt to terminate workers, and thus renege on the implied contract. These workers will suffer a pension loss, just as if they had quit. The industrial restructuring of the American economy over the past decade has substantially altered employment patterns, and many older pension participants have lost their jobs. Such involuntary job changes have imposed pension losses on many workers. The pension penalty facing older workers makes it more difficult for the labor force to respond to changing consumer demands.

Much of the regulatory initiative in the past decade (see chapter 7) can be interpreted as an attempt to reduce the pension cost of changing jobs. This has come during a time of structural change throughout the U.S. economy. As a result of these structural changes, greater emphasis has been placed on the positive value of mobility, which allows the economy to respond to changing economic conditions. It is important for policy makers to realize that policies that reduce the pension loss reduce the value of the defined benefit pension contract and will encourage workers to move away from defined benefit plans. In the long run, the reduced reliance on implicit contracts that reduce turnover can be expected to cause productivity and economic efficiency to decline.

6
Employer Pensions before 1974

Public pensions in the United States are as old as the republic, dating to benefits provided for Revolutionary War veterans. Private employer-provided pensions were introduced in the late nineteenth century and have spread through the economy in the twentieth century. Private pension plans have experienced two periods of relatively rapid growth: 1900 to 1920 and 1940 to 1960. Pension information prior to World War II is based on only a few surveys. More systematic data are available for the postwar years (the more detailed information provided by employers in response to the requirements of ERISA is examined in chapter 7).

Emergence of Private Pensions, 1875 to 1940

Most pension historians credit the American Express Company with establishing the first formal, employer-provided pension plan in 1875.[1] The Baltimore & Ohio Railroad Company followed by introducing a pension in 1880. Only a relatively few additional plans were established before 1900. Early in the twentieth century, however, plans began to spread among large employers in several sectors of the economy. The transportation sector, specifically the railroads, took the lead in establishing company pensions. Public utilities were the next sector to initiate pension plans, followed by banking and insurance firms. Somewhat later, pensions began to spread to the manufacturing sector.[2]

During the first two decades of the twentieth century, pension coverage in the United States expanded. By 1920, pension plans were available in most firms in the railroad, public utility, banking, and mining sectors of the economy, as well as many manufacturing companies engaged in the production of machinery, agricultural implements, chemicals, paints and varnishes, food products, rubber, and paper and printing products.[3]

In 1929, approximately 3.7 million workers were covered by pensions; this represented 14.4 percent of the nonagricultural, privately employed labor force.[4] Over 95 percent of all pension-covered workers were in railroads, public utilities, and manufacturing. Because of high labor turnover rates and long vesting periods, only a small percentage of covered workers ever received retirement benefits.[5] Just as today, these early pension plans were concentrated among large employers. In 1929, two-thirds of all plans were established in firms with 1,000 or more employees. These large plans represented 98 percent of all pension participants.[6] Thus at the turn of the century pensions appear to have been adopted in firms that stood to gain the most from contracting—namely, large firms in which the gains from training were relatively large and the prospects for firm failure were relatively low.

The increase in pension coverage slowed in the 1920s and declined in the 1930s.[7] The adverse economic conditions of the late 1930s made it more difficult to introduce new pensions and led to the failure of unfunded plans.[8] The railroad industry was particularly hard hit. Most railroad firms had not followed a policy of funding their pensions. The declining economic fortunes of these companies and the aging of their work force placed the pension benefits of their employees in jeopardy. The federal government responded with legislation that nationalized these plans.[9] Plan failures in other industries did not receive such federal assistance.

Almost all of these early plans were discretionary pensions, and the employer did not have any legal obligation to provide benefits. Most plans specified that they created no employee rights and that the employer reserved the right to reduce benefits promised to current workers or to retirees already receiving benefits. Thus, these plans clearly were developed as implicit contracts. The worker would receive a retirement benefit on the condition that his performance was satisfactory and that he remained with the firm until retirement.

Most pensions introduced before 1920 tended to be funded solely by the employer (noncontributory plans). More than 70 percent of pension participants were in noncontributory plans.[10] Defined contribution plans were not included in most studies of early pension plans, although one study refers to thirteen "savings plans," which were both money-purchase and profit-sharing plans.[11] The defined contribution plans in this study were adopted between 1907 and 1926.

In 1918, the Teachers Insurance and Annuity Association (TIAA) was established to provide pension coverage for employees of the nation's colleges and universities. TIAA is a large multi-employer, defined contribution plan. It offers fully vested, portable annuities under a contractual, contributory system. TIAA operates as a clearinghouse for the pension contributions of its member institutions and invests and manages the pension fund portfolio. Each person covered by the plan has an individual contract for a retirement annuity that cannot be surrendered for cash. Ten years after its establishment, there were 139 institutions participating in TIAA.[12]

Maturing Pension System, 1940–1974

Plan reports indicate that less than one worker in six in the private, nonagricultural labor force was covered by a pension in 1940. This is similar to the coverage rate for 1929, which indicates that pension coverage had roughly held its own during the depression years.[13] For the next two decades, coverage increased rapidly, from 4.1 million workers in 1940 to 18.7 million in 1960. By then the coverage rate in the private, nonfarm sector had reached 40.8 percent.[14] During the next fifteen years, the number of covered workers continued to increase, primarily because of employment growth in firms that had previously established pension plans and the liberalization of qualification standards for pension coverage.[15]

A 1966 survey of workers aged fifty to sixty-four in private non-farm jobs found that 41 percent of those interviewed were covered by a pension. Workers with longer tenure were more likely to be covered by a pension. The prevailing vesting standards were restrictive, however, and only 52 percent of these older workers who also had twenty or more years of tenure had vested pension rights. The highest coverage rates were in mining, durable manufacturing, transportation and public utilities, and finance.[16]

Further information on pension status in this period comes from the April 1972 Current Population Survey. Respondents were sixteen or older and were employed full-time in the private nonagricultural economy. Coverage in this sample was 47 percent. If we restrict the sample to older workers and compare coverage rates to the 1966 survey, rates are twelve to sixteen percentage points higher in 1972 for workers aged fifty to fifty-nine. This survey also found that only half of the workers with twenty or more years of service had vested pension rights. More than two-thirds of the workers with annual earnings of $10,000 or more were covered by a pension, in comparison with 30 percent of the workers with earnings of $1,000 to $4,999 and 58 percent of the workers earning between $5,000 and $9,999.[17]

Taxation and Pension Regulation

Pension regulation and federal tax policy in the United States have been closely linked since the initiation of federal income taxation in

1913. The expansion of individual and corporate income taxes along with the growth in payroll taxes has provided a strong incentive for employers and employees to negotiate compensation packages that include fringe benefits and deferred compensations that receive preferential tax treatment. In order to qualify for such tax status, pension plans have been required to meet certain guidelines. Over time, these guidelines have become quite comprehensive and have altered the very nature of pension plans.

Before the passage of ERISA in 1974, private pension plans were required to satisfy only a limited set of federal requirements in order to qualify for preferential tax treatment.[18] These requirements were specified in various amendments to the Internal Revenue Code. As the value of favorable treatment increased, the incidence of pension coverage also increased, and plans were modified to comply with the changing provisions of the tax code.

Developments up to 1942. With the institution of a federal income tax in 1913, a question arose as to the tax status of deferred compensation such as pension payments to current retirees and the promise of future pension benefits to current workers. Treasury Decision 2090 of 1914 interpreting Section II.B of the 1913 Revenue Act stated that "amounts paid for pension to retired employees . . . are proper deductions as ordinary and necessary expenses" of employers.[19] Thus, pension benefits paid to current retirees were to be treated as business expenses of the employers and as ordinary income of the retirees.

Up to 1921, employer contributions equal to the normal cost of the pension plan could be deducted as ordinary and necessary business expenses. The normal cost of a pension is the cost of funding benefit liabilities that accrue from work during the current payroll period. Payments to fund past service credits did not receive such favored tax treatment. The common practice was to tax employees for employer contributions at the time of the contribution, unless the possibility of receiving a benefit seemed very doubtful. Income to any pension trust fund was immediately taxable to the employer, the employee, or the trust as a separate entity, depending on provisions of the specific plan.

Tax legislation in 1921 and 1926 altered the tax code so that income earned by stock-bonus and profit-sharing plans and pension trusts were not subject to taxation, and employer contributions to such trusts were not taxable to beneficiaries until they were actually distributed. Employee contributions into pension funds continued to be taxed as current income. Benefit payments to retirees were taxed as

67

current income (only) if they exceeded the employee's own contributions. These changes determined the basic tax status of pensions that still exists today—employer pension contributions are not taxed as current income provided the plan has achieved tax-qualified status. This established the principle that the cost to workers of a dollar of pension wealth would be less than one dollar of after-tax earnings.

Pensions were given favorable tax treatment as long as they were created for the benefit of "some or all of the employees." By including "some" in this phrase, the government allowed firms to establish pension plans that benefited only top management or highly paid employees. This policy allowed firms to develop pension contracts with only a portion of their work force. During this period, there were no guidelines concerning vesting, participation, or funding standards. Thus, in the first third of the twentieth century, government policies did not limit the options available to firms and workers in setting the terms of the pension contract. With long vesting periods and no funding requirements, however, there was considerable uncertainty about the value to the worker of the pension promise. Little systematic evidence exists concerning the proportion of covered workers who eventually received pensions or the number of firms that violated the implicit pension contract during the early years of pension development in the United States.

The Revenue Act of 1938 provided that contributions into pension funds could not be deducted as ordinary business expenses unless it was impossible for management to divert these funds away from the purpose of paying pensions. Therefore, contributions into the pension fund became an irrevocable trust to be used solely for the payment of pension benefits. Prior to this legislation, most company plans did not guarantee any specific benefit to the participants. Funds were controlled by management and could be used for other purposes, as determined by the employer.[20] This act forced firms to set down the terms of the pension contract and to use the funds contributed toward future benefits for that purpose. These changes made the terms of the pension contract more explicit but did not limit the pension penalty that could be imposed on job changers.

1942 Amendments to the Internal Revenue Code. The principal objectives of the 1942 amendments to the Internal Revenue Code were to limit tax subsidies to pensions and to restrict pensions from discriminating in favor of shareholders, management, and highly paid workers. Before 1942, section 165(a) of the Internal Revenue Code had the limited purpose of exempting from taxation the income from pension trusts. The 1942 amendments to this section established criteria to be used to qualify pension plans for preferential tax treatment. To begin with, plans had to be part of a legally binding contract, and written descriptions had to be prepared and communicated to the employees.

In addition, plans had to be for the exclusive benefit of the employees or their beneficiaries and could not discriminate in favor of officers, shareholders, supervisors, or highly compensated employees. A qualified plan had to be designed primarily for pension purposes and not be part of a broader welfare program. The cost of the plan was to be determined by actuarial methods with employers funding the full normal cost of their plans; unfunded past service liabilities for existing plans could not be increased. Other provisions of the act imposed limits on the ordinary and necessary expenses for the plan. Employee contributions, whether voluntary or compulsory, continued to be taxed as current income.

These amendments gave further substance to the pension contract by requiring written plan descriptions and by establishing some minimum funding standards. Limits on discrimination and integration were established. Because of the financial incentives associated with qualifying for favorable tax treatment, plans were modified to meet these requirements.

Legislation from 1942 to 1974. The tax code was extensively revised in 1954, but the amendments basically reaffirmed the 1942 changes. In 1958, the Federal Welfare and Pension Plan Disclosure Act (WPPDA) was passed. The primary objective of this legislation was to require employers to provide plan participants with sufficient information to assess the value of their pensions and to identify any possible malpractice by employers in the management of the pension plan.

The act required administrators of plans with twenty-five or more participants to file a plan description with the Department of Labor every year. These reports had to be available to participants at their request. The premise of this legislation was that if participants and beneficiaries had the complete details of the provisions and financial operations of the plan, they would be able to monitor its administration and prevent abuses without further government intervention.

Although WPPDA outlined the information that these reports had to include, it contained no provisions for uniform reporting forms nor did it give the Department of Labor the authority or responsibility to enforce the act. However, the department was empowered to investigate whether firms had complied with the disclosure requirements.

The Self-Employed Individuals Tax Retirement Act of 1962 provided the structure that enabled self-employed persons to establish

Keogh retirement plans. Contributions to these plans were to be tax deductible. Contributions were limited to $2,500, or 10 percent annually of earned income. Earnings from plan assets accumulated tax-free until they were distributed to the participants.

Summary of the Pre-ERISA Period

During the twentieth century, pensions have spread throughout the economy. The growing demand for old age pensions reflects the increasing life expectancy of workers and rising real wages. As earnings have increased, workers have become better able to defer a portion of their income to support themselves during retirement. The number of years in retirement have increased because of earlier retirement and longer life spans. With longer retirement periods, greater savings are needed to provide income after earnings cease. Company-sponsored savings plans paid for in the form of lower earnings offer opportunities for accumulating funds to finance the retirement years.

In the presence of increased demand for earlier retirement, a system of company pensions would likely have developed in the United States in the absence of tax incentives. However, we can offer no specific information to determine why workers preferred defined benefit plans to defined contribution plans. These workers probably were assessing the same risk factors as today's workers (see chapters 2 and 3) as well as the relative price of each type of pension. These comparisons convinced workers that their interests were best served by defined benefit plans.

The value to firms of reduced employee turnover increased during this period because the jobs they offered required higher skills and this involved greater hiring and training costs. As the cost of turnover rose, firms attempted to limit quits. As noted earlier, defined benefit plans provide the means to limit worker mobility and thus to reduce these costs. The changes in production technology that were occurring in the United States gave firms the economic incentive to adopt defined benefit pension plans instead of defined contribution plans.

The rapid growth in pension coverage from 1940 to 1960 was stimulated by a variety of other events. First, the 1942 amendments to the Internal Revenue Code clarified and expanded the tax treatment of pensions and prohibited firms from establishing pensions solely for corporate officers, highly paid workers, and stockholders. Second, the wartime stabilization policy made it easier to increase less observable fringe benefits rather than cash wages. Third, the 1949 Inland Steel decision determined that collective bargaining requirements for wages and compensation under the National Labor Relations Act included the mandatory bargaining for pension benefits. This action altered union attitudes toward seeking retirement benefits through employer-operated pension funds, and led unions to push for expanded pension coverage and to accept defined benefit plans. By requiring employers to bargain over pensions, the decision also provided unions with a framework for expressing their demands for pensions.[21]

Perhaps the most important reason for the rapid expansion of pension coverage during the 1940s and 1950s was the dramatic rise in federal income tax rates and the proportion of persons subject to these taxes. The marginal federal personal income tax rate paid by the median taxpayer rose from 4.4 percent in 1940 to 23.0 percent in 1945 and remained at approximately 20 percent thereafter. The marginal corporate tax rate paid by large firms increased from 24.0 percent in 1940 to 40.0 percent in 1945 and then to approximately 50 percent in subsequent years. In addition, the proportion of persons required to actually pay income taxes rose from 13 percent of those filing income tax returns in 1940 to 65 percent in 1945.[22]

Pensions were not only affected by income taxes but also by the social insurance legislation of the 1930s and its subsequent expansion. The retirement, disability, and health insurance components of social security are financed by payroll taxes, which are levied only on cash earnings. Pension contributions permanently avoid these payroll taxes. The increased coverage of the social insurance programs and their increasing tax rates added to the tax incentives that encouraged employers to offer pension plans and to have their pension plans qualified for tax purposes.[23]

The preferential tax treatment accorded pension contributions and earnings on pension funds significantly reduced costs to firms and workers of negotiating this form of compensation. The course of development of the private pension system during this time indicates that plans were modified to achieve and maintain qualified status. Most plans were not funded during the time that employer contributions and earnings on plan assets were taxed as income to either the employer, the employee, or the pension trust. After the 1920s, when preferential tax status was accorded employer contributions and plan earnings, plans increasingly shifted from pay-as-you-go to funded plans. Plans were financed primarily by employer contributions instead of employee contributions because employee contributions could only be made with after-tax dollars. These early regulations placed only minor restrictions on the provisions of pension plans.

Up to 1974, pensions plans were clearly shaped in part by government tax policies and requirements that pensions achieve qualified status. These qualifying provisions set general guidelines for pensions by requiring employers to provide information on plan provisions. They also made it difficult for firms to recover pension contributions. However, the specific terms of participation, vesting, retirement ages, and benefit levels were to be negotiated by the firm and its workers. The economic agents involved with the pension contract retained considerable flexibility on these issues. Taxation of employee contributions provided a strong incentive for funding pensions solely by employer contributions.

There are no comprehensive data to indicate the preferred types of plans during this period, although one study has constructed a pseudo time series of plan type coverage by sorting plans in operation in 1981 by their year of adoption.[24] The results show no trend toward greater use of primary defined contribution plans before 1974; however, defined contribution plans did gain considerable ground as supplemental plans to existing defined benefit plans. The majority of the new defined contribution plans in the 1950s and 1960s were of the profit-sharing type, and most of these plans were adopted by small employers.[25]

The two primary objectives of federal pension policy during this period were to encourage the spread of pensions through tax subsidies and to prevent companies from using the tax subsidies solely for the benefit of managers, stockholders, and highly paid executives. If the development of the pension system is measured against these objectives, government policy was relatively successful and required only a minimum amount of interference with the pension contract.

Despite the lack of data on pension coverage by plan type, it is certain that defined benefit plans were the preferred choice for primary coverage during this relatively unregulated period. Thus, when workers and firms negotiated pensions based on the gains and costs of each plan type, they generally chose defined benefit plans. Regulations restricting plan provisions were rare, and the government's principal role was to provide tax incentives. These tax incentives encouraged firms to adopt pensions but seem to have been neutral concerning the choice of plan type.

7
Comprehensive Pension Regulation and the Changing Structure of Pensions, 1974 to 1988

The passage of the Employee Retirement Income Security Act in 1974 represented a fundamental shift in public pension policy. This comprehensive legislation established guidelines for operating pension funds and set specific requirements for various pension plan provisions. ERISA altered pension regulation by setting standards for participant rights to future pension benefits, regulating the operation of the pension fund itself, and mandating pension insurance for defined benefit plans. It required firms to revise their pension plans, reducing the range of choice on key plan provisions, and increased the reporting requirements. For plan participants, ERISA reduced the pension cost of changing jobs and the uncertainty about receiving benefits. For firms, ERISA reduced the value of the defined benefit contract, and increased the cost of offering these plans.

Since 1974 the federal government has enacted new pension regulations almost annually. These new regulations have continued to raise the cost of offering defined benefit plans in comparison with defined contribution plans and have made it more difficult for workers and firms to enter into productivity-enhancing contracts.

Employee Retirement Income Security Act

The full impact of ERISA cannot be understood without examining its central provisions that have important implications for workers and firms. A brief description of these key provisions is presented below.

Vesting and Participation Requirements. Before ERISA, many plans required relatively long periods of service before a worker became eligible to participate in the plan. In defined benefit plans, it was common practice to exclude young workers (under thirty years of age) from the plan, and to insist on five or ten years of service before allowing a worker to participate. Under ERISA, eligibility has been extended to all employees who are at least twenty-five and have completed one year of service.

Once participation had begun, most defined benefit plans in the pre-ERISA years required relatively long, continuous service before a worker's benefits became vested. Some firms actually required workers to remain with them until retirement before vesting their pensions benefits. ERISA required that all plans meet one of three vesting standards: (1) 100 percent vesting after ten years of service, (2) 25 percent vesting after five years of service, with additional vesting accruing at a rate of 5 percent per year for the next five years and 10 percent per year for the following five years so that the worker was 100 percent vested after fifteen years, and (3) the rule of forty-five, whereby the worker was 50 percent vested when his age plus years of service equaled forty-five, with additional vesting accruing at a rate of 10 percent per year for the next five years. ERISA also established guidelines for what constituted a break in service and the minimum number of hours of work necessary to achieve a year of credited service. These mandated changes forced virtually all defined benefit plans to rewrite their vesting and participation rules. As noted in chapter 2, defined contribution plans have historically had relatively short vesting and participation requirements. Therefore, the ERISA restrictions had less of an impact on defined contribution plans.

Insurance and Funding Standards. Under pre-ERISA tax legislation, funds placed into a pension were redeemable by the firm only if all liabilities had been paid. However, if the plan was terminated because a firm went bankrupt and there were insufficient assets to pay vested benefits, workers and retirees might receive sharply reduced benefits or none at all. Therefore, pension benefits were secure only to the extent that there were enough assets to pay future pension benefits.

After ERISA established the Pension Benefit Guaranty Corporation (PBGC), the payment of vested legal pension benefits under defined benefit plans was guaranteed, even if the plan was terminated and assets were insufficient. There is, however, a maximum benefit guaranteed by the PBGC. When a plan is terminated and has insufficient assets to pay vested benefits, the PBGC can hold the sponsoring company liable for the underfunding up to an amount equal to 30 percent of the company's net worth. All single-employer defined benefit plans are required to pay a uniform premium of $1 per year per participant to support this insurance system. Defined contribution plans that are by their nature fully funded do not have to purchase this pension insurance.

The mandatory purchase of insurance raised the direct cost of defined benefit plans. The impact of the insurance premium on firm costs is somewhat offset by the lower wages that workers may be willing to accept for participating in a given pension contract with lower risks of pension losses. Since the PBGC premium was not risk related, the cost to low-risk plans exceeded the value of this insurance to the plan participants. The costs to these plans were increased by the pension insurance requirement. High-risk plans were actually subsidized.

In an effort to ensure adequate funding, ERISA imposed new funding standards and instituted restrictions on the evaluation of pension funds. Prior to 1974, firms were required to make annual payments equal to the normal costs of the plan for the year plus the interest on their unfunded prior service costs. Under ERISA, employer contributions had to equal annual benefit accruals plus liabilities from employees' prior service amortized over not more than forty years, plus any new liabilities resulting from the new plan or benefit liberalizations in old plans amortized over thirty years. Methods of asset evaluation and actuarial assumptions were specified in the legislation. These requirements substantially increased annual pension contributions to defined benefit plans for many firms. Defined contribution plans typically were not affected by these funding rules.

Prior to 1974, retirement benefits or employer contributions in qualified pension plans were not subject to any limits. ERISA established a benefit limit for defined benefit plans of the lesser of $75,000 per year or 100 percent of the retiree's average earnings during the three preceding years. Employer contributions to defined contribution plans were limited to the lesser of $25,000 or 25 percent of compensation. Both dollar limits were indexed to the Consumer Price Index (CPI).

Reporting Rules. ERISA expanded and strengthened the reporting and disclosure rules for pensions. One rule calls for a written description of the plan, copies of which must be made available to all employees. The plan administrator must furnish all participants and beneficiaries with a summary of the plan's essential features and provisions, which is known as the summary plan description (SPD). Regulations specify what information is to be included in the SPD.

Plan administrators are also required to file an annual report with the Internal Revenue Service within seven months after the end of the plan year. All plans with 100 participants or more are required to complete Form 5500, whereas smaller plans can file somewhat simpler forms. These forms indicate plan type, various plan provisions, number of participants and beneficiaries, and financial status of the plan.

Individual Retirement and Keogh Accounts. ERISA authorized Individual Retirement Accounts (IRAs) for persons not covered by either an employer pension plan or a Keogh plan. Beginning in 1975, persons could set up an IRA and make tax-deductible contributions equal to 15 percent of earnings up to a maximum of $1,500 annually. IRA earnings were allowed to accumulate tax-free until distribution. Title II of ERISA raised Keogh deductible contributions to the lesser of 15 percent of earnings or $7,500 per year.

Post-ERISA Regulations

ERISA contained a wide variety of regulations governing the adoption and operation of qualified pension plans. No other major regulations concerning defined benefit plans were introduced during the 1970s. However, several changes in the tax code influenced various types of defined contribution plans. The Tax Reduction Act of 1975 gave a tax credit to employers for contributions to employee stock option plans that met certain standards. The credit for these Tax Reduction Act Stock Option Plans (TRASOPs) was equal to 1 percent of new capital investment or the amount of the contributions to the plan. The Tax Reform Act of 1976 extended TRASOPs tax credits to matching employee contributions.

The Revenue Act of 1978 created simplified employee pensions (SEPs) to allow small employers to establish employer-financed pensions similar to IRAs for eligible workers. Annual contributions were limited to the lesser of $7,500 or 15 percent of compensation. This legislation also provided for the tax-deferred rollover of pension funds from one tax-qualified plan to another. Although these changes in the tax code increased options for defined contribution plans, the new options were aimed primarily at small firms. Each year since 1980, the government has made some modifications to the tax codes and regulations governing pension plans.[1] Key aspects of these changes are summarized in the following paragraphs.

Economic Recovery Tax Act of 1981. Under this legislation, voluntary employee contributions (up to $2,000 per year) to tax-qualified pension plans, a section 403(b) annuity, or an SEP became tax-deductible. As a result, these types of defined contribution plans became more desirable. Tax-deferred status was not extended to mandatory employee contributions. The act also created payroll-based tax credit employee stock ownership plans (PAYSOPs) as a substitute for TRASOPs. It extended eligibility for individual retirement accounts to all wage earners, including those covered by an employer pension, and contribution limits were increased to $2,000 per year. Deductible Keogh contributions were raised to $15,000. These provisions expanded the options available to workers and firms wishing to establish defined contribution plans.

Tax Equity and Fiscal Responsibility Act of 1982. This act reduced the maximum annual benefit under a defined benefit plan from 100 percent of compensation (but not exceeding $136,425 a year) to the lower of 100 percent of compensation or $90,000 per year. In addition, the maximum annual contribution under a defined contribution plan was reduced from $45,475 or 25 percent of earnings to $30,000 or 25 percent of earnings. Contribution limits to SEP accounts were raised to $30,000. These new limits were to be frozen until 1986, when they were to be reindexed to the CPI. This act also introduced so-called top-heavy rules, which are special standards applied to plans in which 60 percent of pension benefits are earmarked for key employees.

The allowable difference in contribution rates above and below the social security wage base used in integrated defined contribution plans was reduced. Previously, contributions on earnings in excess of the social security wage base could exceed contributions on earnings below the base by up to 7 percent. The new differential was set equal to the employer's payroll tax for Old Age Survivors and Disability Insurance (OASDI). At the time, the tax rate was 5.4 percent.

The legislation disallowed employer contributions to defined benefit plans if they were going to be used to fund anticipated future cost-of-living adjustments. If employers are unable to plan directly for future increases in retiree benefits, postretirement adjustments will become smaller and less frequent. The effect of this legislation is not yet known. If it increases the inflation risk in defined benefit plans, it may encourage more workers to shift to defined contribution plans.

Deficit Reduction Act of 1984. This act kept the ceiling on maximum benefits in defined benefit plans at $90,000 and on employer contributions to defined contribution plans at $30,000. Beginning in 1988, the limits were to be reindexed to the CPI. Modifications were made in the required timing of distributions, SEP employee deductions on employer contributions, IRA rollover provisions, and contributions to 401(k) plans.

Retirement Equity Act of 1984. The objective of this act was to ensure that workers covered by pensions would eventually receive benefits. It reduced the maximum age for pension participation from twenty-five to twenty-one, set limits on what represented a break in service, and granted nonvested employees leaving a firm and subsequently rehired within five years credit for previous service. New protection was granted to workers temporarily away from the job because of maternity and paternity leave. Pension plans were required to provide a joint survivorship benefit unless waived by the spouse and to include a preretirement survivor provision.

Consolidated Omnibus Budget Reconciliation Act of 1986. This act increased the annual PBGC premium to $8.50 per participant. The premium continued to be uniform across all plans and thus was not made a function of the funding status of the plan.

Tax Reform Act of 1986. This act lowered maximum contributions to 401(k) plans to $7,000 and limited the use of Individual Retirement Accounts by persons covered by a qualified pension. Effective in 1989 vesting requirements were to be reduced so that workers could be granted either 100 percent vesting after five years of service or 20 percent vesting after three years of service with 100 percent vesting after seven years. Additional taxes were placed on preretirement lump-sum distributions, and social security integration standards were modified. Tighter pension plan standards and tax penalties were placed on early withdrawals by workers and on firms receiving excess assets from plan terminations in an effort to ensure that deferred income was used for retirement purposes.

Amendments to the Age Discrimination in Employment Act of 1986. These amendments to ADEA outlawed mandatory retirement requirements at any age in most jobs. The 1978 ADEA amendments precluded mandatory retirement prior to age seventy, but before that, many pension-covered jobs also included mandatory retirement at age sixty-five as a component of the employment contract.

Omnibus Budget Reconciliation Act of 1986. This legislation required that pensions continue to allow contributions or benefit accruals for employees who remain employed past the normal retirement age.

Pension Protection Act of 1987 and the Omnibus Budget Reconciliation Act of 1987. These acts raised the per capita insurance payment to the PBGC to $16 and required additional payments for underfunded plans up to a maximum payment of $50 per participant. They also placed new limits on overfunded plans and on access to funds in the event of plan termination. Funding standards were made more restrictive, primarily for defined benefit plans, and a range of interest rates was established for plans to use when valuing current liabilities. The overfunding limit of 150 percent of legal vested liabilities means that firms cannot make new tax-free contributions to plans that are overfunded in their legal liabilities. Therefore, administrators wanting to fund an ongoing plan for projected benefits may be prevented from doing so. Rapid swings in interest rates may push firms over the full funding limits and thus prohibit firms from making any new contributions into the fund. By limiting tax-deferred contributions, these policies have introduced another form of uncertainty for sponsors.

Evaluation of Regulatory Change

ERISA established guidelines specifying what provisions were required if pensions were to qualify for favorable tax treatment. These guidelines reduced the uncertainty surrounding the disbursement of benefits. At the same time, virtually all defined benefit plans had to be revised, and the flexibility associated with offering defined benefit pension plans was substantially reduced. As a result, the scope of permissible pension contracts was reduced, as were the potential gains, while the costs of offering such a contract were increased. The costs of reporting and operating a pension plan were also increased.

These changes affected defined benefit and defined contribution plans differently and accelerated the movement away from defined benefit plans and toward defined contribution plans. Before 1974, for example, 81 percent of defined contribution plans had already met ERISA standards for vesting.[2] These plans also tended to have low requirements for participation, were fully funded by definition, and were irrevocable trusts by law. In contrast, only 19 percent of defined benefit plans prior to the passage of ERISA had vesting standards comparable to those mandated by ERISA. It has been estimated that prior to 1974, 40 percent of all participants in defined benefit plans could not achieve vesting until retirement. In addition, many defined benefit plans were substantially unfunded. These plans were faced with significant increases in annual pension contributions.[3]

The regulatory changes adopted since 1974 have reduced the flexibility of contracts that enabled firms and workers to develop pension contracts specific to their situations and have foreclosed the offering of certain types of pension contracts. The effect of the current regulations has been to increase the probability that workers covered by defined benefit pensions will receive their pensions. The value to workers of the regulatory changes accrue primarily to mobile workers through lower vesting and participation standards.

Prior to ERISA, few firms violated the implied pension contract by systematically firing older workers before they were vested or by having insufficient assets to pay benefits. If widespread employer fraud was not present, then the gains to workers from the regulatory initiatives would have been more apparent than real.

ERISA and the regulatory initiatives that followed have raised the cost of providing defined benefit pensions and have lowered the value of the pension contract. In the wake of these regulations, the incidence of defined benefit coverage has declined. These post-ERISA regulations have increased the administrative and reporting costs for all pensions, especially for defined benefit plans. They have reduced the value of defined benefit pension contracts to firms, thereby limiting their options to use pensions as incentives to influence employee turnover and retirement. This means that the cost of a dollar of future pension benefits to the worker in terms of forgone earnings has risen. In response to these changes, fewer workers and firms will want to pay the extra costs associated with defined benefit plans.

In contrast to their considerable effects on the costs and benefits of establishing and maintaining a defined benefit plan, the regulations have had much less impact on defined contribution plans. This is due to the fact that most defined contribution plans are fully funded and are not required to purchase PBGC insurance. Changes in the vesting and participation standards also have affected defined contribution plans to a lesser degree, since historically they have had shorter waiting periods than defined benefit plans. In addition, changes in the tax code accompanying the regulatory changes have increased the options for providing defined contribution plans.

Pension regulation has continued to evolve during the 1980s. Firms have been faced with a changing regulatory environment in which the acceptable pension rules have been altered. As a result, firms have had to modify their plans frequently. Costs associated with these modifications include the higher costs of the new plan and payments to actuaries and lawyers to rewrite plans to conform to the new regulations. Firms with existing defined benefit plans or those considering new plans must consider costs that future changes in regulation may introduce when they are deciding which type of plan to select.

Regulations have changed frequently during the 1980s owing to the large federal budget deficit and the desire of policy makers to find additional revenues. This search has regularly turned to employee benefits. As a result, tax and general fiscal policy has been influencing pension policy. These tax-driven policies have been aimed primarily at funding rules associated with defined benefit plans, although maximum contributions to defined contribution plans have also been lowered.

Declining Use of Defined Benefit Pensions—Data from the 5500 Forms

The decline in the relative use of defined benefit plans in the private sector of the economy can be illustrated using data from the 5500 reporting forms for 1977 to 1985. The pension data are limited to primary pension plans with 100 or more participants. We do not focus on small plans where the use of defined contribution plans is the greatest. Nor do we include supplementary plans. Related evidence suggests that supplementary defined contribution plans have spread rapidly throughout the economy over the past two decades. The question is, to what extent have defined contribution plans replaced defined benefit plans as the primary mechanism for providing retirement benefits for workers in firms with at least 100 employees?

Data from the 5500 forms clearly indicate a dramatic increase in the use of defined contribution plans in the post-ERISA period. In 1977 there were 15,652 primary defined benefit plans with more than 100 participants covering 20.3 million workers (table 7–1). This meant that 77.7 percent of all primary plans were defined benefit plans, and these plans covered 88.9 percent of the participants. In contrast, there were only 4,384 defined contribution plans covering 2.12 million workers.

Table 7–1 reveals a strong trend toward greater use of defined contribution plans between 1977 and 1985. By 1985, the number of defined benefit plans had risen to 23,174 and participants to 26.7 million. However, this represented only 64.7 percent of the primary plans and 78.7 percent of the participants in these plans. During this period, the number of defined benefit plans and the number of participants in these plans continued to increase but at a much slower pace than the expansion of defined contribution plans. Most of the growth in defined benefit plans occurred before 1980. Between 1983 and 1985, the number of defined benefit plans actually fell in absolute terms.

These data have been sorted by industry, employer size, and by the effective date of the plan. By examining the trend within these categories, we can determine if the trend toward greater use of de-

TABLE 7-1

Number of Primary Plans and Active Participants, by Plan Type, 1977–1985

Plan Type	Plans				Participants (millions)			
	1977	1980	1983	1985	1977	1980	1983	1985
Defined benefit	15,652	22,010	23,264	23,174	20.3	26.4	26.0	26.7
	(77.7)	(74.7)	(70.3)	(64.7)	(88.9)	(87.1)	(82.0)	(78.7)
Defined contribution	4,394	7,271	9,623	12,427	2.2	3.6	5.3	6.9
	(21.8)	(24.7)	(29.1)	(34.7)	(9.9)	(11.9)	(16.9)	(20.4)
Other[a]	101	187	209	231	0.3	0.3	0.4	0.3
	(0.5)	(0.6)	(0.6)	(0.6)	(1.2)	(0.9)	(1.1)	(0.9)
Total	20,137	29,468	33,096	35,832	22.8	30.3	31.7	33.9
	(100.0)	(100.0)	(100.0)	(100.0)	(100.0)	(100.0)	(100.0)	(100.0)

Note: Firms having no primary plans of 100 or more participants and tax-exempt organizations are excluded. The numbers in parentheses represent the percentage of column totals.

a. These plans include defined benefit plans based partly on the balance of separate accounts of the participant (code section 414(b)), annuity arrangements of certain exempt organizations (code section 403(b)(1)), custodial accounts for regulated investment company stock (code section 403(b)(7)), and pension plans utilizing individual retirement accounts or annuities (described in code section 408) as the sole funding vehicle for providing benefits.

Source: 5500 Tax Reporting Forms, 1977–1985.

fined contribution plans is limited to specific industries or types of firms. Tables 7–2 and 7–3 report the number of plans and number of participants covered by each plan type within each of the nine major industrial classifications. In 1977, more than 80 percent of all primary plans in mining, manufacturing, and transportation and communications were defined benefit plans. However, in the trade sectors of the economy, slightly more than 50 percent of the plans were defined benefit plans. Owing to the greater use of defined benefit plans by larger firms, more than 79 percent of all participants in primary plans in each of the industries were in defined benefit plans.

Substantial changes occurred in the private pension system between 1977 and 1985. The proportion of primary plans that were defined benefit plans declined in every sector. In manufacturing, defined benefit plans dropped from 83.1 percent of all plans in 1977 to 74.0 percent in 1985, while the proportion of participants in the defined benefit plans fell from 91.4 to 84.4 percent. To control for a decline in steel and automobile employment, the manufacturing sector is divided into ferrous metal, motor vehicles, and other. The proportion of pension plans that are defined benefit plans in each of these subsectors declined, as did the proportion of pension participants covered by defined benefit plans. Thus, the decline in the use of defined benefit plans in the manufacturing sector is not due solely to reduced employment in steel and automobile firms.

TABLE 7–2

DISTRIBUTION OF PRIMARY PLANS, BY INDUSTRY AND PLAN TYPE,
1977–1985

Plan Type	Defined Benefit				Defined Contribution			
	1977	1980	1983	1985	1977	1980	1983	1985
Agriculture	103	142	174	170	38	66	110	124
	(72.5)	(68.3)	(61.3)	(57.4)	(26.8)	(31.7)	(38.7)	(41.9)
Mining	296	426	458	411	63	115	196	223
	(82.0)	(78.2)	(69.8)	(64.8)	(17.5)	(21.1)	(29.9)	(35.2)
Construction	862	1,323	1,054	1,229	279	579	646	908
	(75.1)	(68.5)	(61.3)	(57.3)	(24.3)	(30.0)	(37.6)	(42.4)
Manufacturing	8,849	12,119	12,539	11,807	1,759	2,719	3,328	4,114
	(83.1)	(81.4)	(78.8)	(74.0)	(16.5)	(18.3)	(20.9)	(25.8)
Ferrous metal	329	418	405	350	30	35	40	62
	(91.1)	(92.1)	(90.8)	(84.7)	(8.3)	(7.7)	(9.0)	(15.0)
Motor vehicles	329	410	417	433	24	40	53	72
	(93.2)	(91.4)	(88.7)	(85.6)	(6.8)	(8.9)	(11.3)	(14.2)
Other	8,191	11,291	11,717	11,024	1,705	2,644	3,235	3,980
	(82.5)	(80.7)	(78.1)	(73.3)	(17.2)	(18.9)	(21.6)	(26.5)
Transportation, communications	979	1,224	1,273	1,188	208	278	400	507
	(81.4)	(80.7)	(75.3)	(69.8)	(17.3)	(18.3)	(23.7)	(29.8)
Wholesale trade	583	842	931	904	440	688	840	1,031
	(56.7)	(54.7)	(52.2)	(46.6)	(42.8)	(44.7)	(47.1)	(53.1)
Retail trade	591	912	937	922	531	849	1,122	1,335
	(52.5)	(51.5)	(45.4)	(40.8)	(47.2)	(47.9)	(54.4)	(59.0)
Finance, insurance, real estate	1,525	1,888	2,138	2,011	471	558	791	1,058
	(76.0)	(76.7)	(72.6)	(65.3)	(23.5)	(22.7)	(26.9)	(34.4)
Services	1,864	2,756	3,101	3,061	595	1,204	1,834	2,373
	(75.2)	(68.8)	(62.1)	(55.7)	(24.0)	(30.0)	(36.7)	(43.2)

NOTE: Firms with no primary plans of 100 or more participants and tax-exempt organizations are excluded. Figures in parentheses indicate the percentage of plans in each industry. For a given year, these values do not add to 100 percent because other primary plans are not shown in the table. For a description of these other plan types, see table 7–1.
SOURCE: 5500 Tax Reporting Forms, 1977–1985.

TABLE 7–3

DISTRIBUTION OF PARTICIPANTS IN PRIMARY PLANS, BY INDUSTRY AND
PLAN TYPE, 1977–1985

(hundreds of thousands)

Plan Type	Defined Benefit				Defined Contribution			
	1977	1980	1983	1985	1977	1980	1983	1985
Agriculture	0.7	1.0	1.0	1.1	0.1	0.2	0.4	0.6
	(87.9)	(82.4)	(72.4)	(65.4)	(12.0)	(17.6)	(27.6)	(34.4)
Mining	2.2	4.4	5.2	3.8	0.3	0.6	0.8	1.2
	(86.3)	(88.3)	(87.0)	(76.3)	(13.4)	(11.5)	(12.8)	(23.7)
Construction	15.1	22.9	15.7	16.9	1.5	4.6	4.9	7.0
	(90.9)	(82.6)	(75.3)	(70.7)	(8.8)	(16.6)	(23.6)	(29.2)
Manufacturing	105.9	128.4	121.2	115.2	9.1	11.0	14.9	19.2
	(91.4)	(91.0)	(87.9)	(84.4)	(7.8)	(7.8)	(10.8)	(14.0)
Ferrous metal	5.7	6.1	4.7	3.6	0.1	0.2	0.2	0.3
	(97.7)	(97.2)	(95.2)	(91.4)	(1.7)	(2.7)	(4.8)	(8.6)
Motor vehicles	14.1	14.3	12.2	11.9	0.1	0.1	0.23	0.2
	(99.2)	(99.1)	(98.4)	(97.5)	(0.8)	(0.9)	(1.6)	(1.9)
Other	86.1	108.0	104.3	99.7	8.9	10.7	14.5	18.6
	(89.8)	(89.7)	(86.6)	(82.9)	(9.3)	(8.9)	(12.0)	(15.5)
Transportation	29.5	36.3	34.3	32.3	2.6	2.8	3.5	5.4
communications	(91.5)	(92.4)	(90.1)	(85.6)	(8.0)	(7.2)	(9.2)	(14.2)
Wholsale trade	4.8	5.7	6.1	5.6	1.3	1.9	2.5	2.9
	(79.7)	(74.7)	(70.6)	(65.4)	(20.8)	(25.0)	(28.6)	(34.5)
Retail trade	14.8	19.6	19.1	24.5	3.0	5.4	9.9	11.2
	(82.8)	(78.3)	(64.7)	(68.6)	(17.1)	(21.4)	(33.6)	(68.6)
Finance,								
insurance	15.0	19.4	23.6	24.9	2.6	4.1	6.6	6.6
real estate	(79.0)	(81.8)	(77.9)	(78.9)	(13.8)	(17.3)	(21.8)	(20.9)
Services	14.5	24.1	26.1	29.2	2.0	4.8	8.5	11.9
	(86.4)	(82.2)	(74.7)	(70.5)	(11.8)	(16.5)	(24.3)	(28.8)

NOTE: Firms with no primary plans of 100 or more participants and tax-exempt organizations are excluded. The figures in parentheses indicate the percentage of participants in each industry. For a given year, these values do not add to 100 percent because other primary plans are not shown in this table. For a description of these other plan types, see table 7–1.
SOURCE: 5500 Tax Reporting Forms, 1977–1985.

When each industry is examined separately, we find a decline in the relative use of defined benefit plans and in the proportion of participants covered by these plans. Absolute declines in defined benefit coverage between 1980 and 1985 are recorded in mining, manufacturing, transportation and communications, and wholesale trade. The tables also report a corresponding increase in the use of primary defined contribution plans. There are large absolute increases in defined contribution plans in virtually every sector of the economy.

When plans are sorted by the number of participants, we again find a strong movement toward greater use of defined contribution plans. Table 7–4 reports the number of plans in five size categories. As expected, larger plans are much more likely to be defined benefit plans. In 1977, 65.7 percent of plans with 100 to 149 participants and 72.9 percent of plans with 150 to 249 participants were defined benefit plans. This compares with more than 80 percent of plans with 250 to 999 participants and more than 90 percent of plans with 1,000 or more participants.[4]

In each of these size categories, there is a substantial decline in the proportion of plans that are defined benefit over the eight years, but the decline decreases with plan size. The greatest decline occurs among plans with fewer than 250 participants. In each of the two smaller size categories, the proportion of plans that were defined benefit plans declined by almost fifteen percentage points, and defined benefit plans actually decreased in absolute number between

TABLE 7–4

SIZE DISTRIBUTION OF PRIMARY PLANS, 1977–1985

Size	Defined Benefit				Defined Contribution			
	1977	1980	1983	1985	1977	1980	1983	1985
100–149	2,664	3,706	3,991	3,605	1,390	2,142	2,815	3,480
	(65.7)	(63.4)	(58.6)	(50.9)	(34.4)	(36.6)	(41.4)	(49.1)
150–249	3,452	4,964	5,395	5,271	1,282	2,258	2,984	3,780
	(72.9)	(68.7)	(64.4)	(58.2)	(27.1)	(31.3)	(25.6)	(41.8)
250–499	3,713	5,268	5,380	5,418	917	1,573	2,070	2,650
	(80.2)	(77.0)	(72.2)	(67.2)	(19.8)	(23.0)	(27.8)	(29.1)
500–999	2,499	3,470	3,606	3,676	432	686	903	1,288
	(85.3)	(88.9)	(80.0)	(74.1)	(14.7)	(17.6)	(20.0)	(25.9)
1,000 or more	3,308	4,570	4,855	5,166	358	610	847	1,222
	(90.2)	(88.2)	(85.1)	(80.9)	(10.9)	(11.8)	(14.8)	(19.1)

NOTE: Firms with no primary plans of 100 or more participants and tax-exempt organizations are excluded. Figures in parentheses indicate the percentage of total plans by plan type that are in the size category. For a given year, these values do not add to 100 percent because other primary plans are not shown in this table. For a description of these other plan types, see table 7–1.
SOURCE: 5500 Tax Reporting Forms, 1977–1985.

1983 and 1985. In larger plans, relative use of defined benefit plans declined by as much as thirteen percentage points among plans having between 250 and 499 participants and to as low as nine percentage points among plans with more than 1,000 participants. Note also that in every size category shown in table 7–4 the absolute increase in the number of plans between 1980 and 1985 is greater for defined contribution than for defined benefit plans. Even among plans with 1,000 or more participants, the increase in defined contribution plans (612) was greater than the increase in defined benefit plans (596).

Still another way to illustrate the trend toward greater use of defined contribution plans is to examine the effective date of all plans operating in 1985. In this analysis we are considering plans that operate at a particular point in time and therefore are interested in the pattern of initiation and termination of different plan types over time. Tables 7–5 and 7–6 report the number of defined contribution plans still in effect in 1985 that were started in each of six time periods under consideration, ranging from before 1941 to the 1980s, and the proportion of all plans started during each period that were defined contribution plans. These data are reported for each industry by two size categories.

For smaller plans (those with fewer than 1,000 participants in 1985), there was an increase over time in the proportion of plans that are defined contribution plans (table 7–5). This is also true for the proportion of participants covered by the plans started during the specified periods. For example, among small manufacturing firms, less than one-quarter of the plans started in the three decades prior to ERISA were defined contribution plans. In the five years between 1974 and 1979, the proportion of new plans in these firms that were defined contribution plans rose to one-third, and between 1980 and 1985 it increased to almost one-half. Similar changes are observed in other sectors such as mining, transportation, and finance, which traditionally have relied heavily on defined benefit plans.

A similar trend is observed among large plans (table 7–6). Before 1974, less than 12 percent of all large plans started in manufacturing were defined contribution plans. However, the proportion of new plans that were defined contribution plans increased to 27.2 percent between 1974 and 1979 and to 37.1 percent between 1980 and 1985. New defined contribution plans in this latter period covered 46.6 percent of the participants in large plans in manufacturing started during this time. Thus, defined contribution plans represented more than one-third of all new large primary plans started in manufacturing in the first half of the 1980s, and these plans covered almost one-

TABLE 7–5

New Plans in Firms with Fewer than 1,000 Employees That Were
Defined Contribution Plans, by Industry, from
before 1941 to 1985
(percent)

Industry	Before 1941	1942–1953	1954–1963	1964–1973	1974–1979	1980–1985
Agriculture						
Plans[a]	0.0	12.0	29.0	40.0	52.6	74.5
Participants[b]	0.0	11.0	31.9	42.7	56.5	73.0
Number of starts[c]	7	25	31	75	57	51
Mining						
Plans	0.0	15.0	30.0	19.5	50.0	54.2
Participants	0.0	20.4	33.1	17.6	46.1	49.6
Number of starts	4	40	70	123	156	144
Construction						
Plans	0.0	30.6	25.3	31.7	77.2	81.8
Participants	0.0	26.5	20.6	30.2	77.1	80.8
Number of starts	3	49	336	625	237	302
Manufacturing						
Plans	13.0	13.6	18.3	22.4	34.7	46.1
Participants	20.0	15.8	19.7	22.8	35.2	43.1
Number of starts	108	1220	2555	4156	2629	2639
Transportation						
Plans	5.9	8.3	14.9	30.9	50.2	66.8
Participants	3.4	11.0	15.5	30.1	49.3	59.4
Number of starts	17	120	248	304	243	250
Wholesale trade						
Plans	40.0	35.0	51.1	52.3	60.6	69.8
Participants	64.0	29.9	51.2	53.2	56.6	64.6
Number of starts	5	140	329	593	378	318
Retail trade						
Plans	100.0	42.4	60.5	61.6	71.7	72.9
Participants	100.0	41.2	63.5	59.3	70.6	71.9
Number of starts	3	92	256	636	417	376
Finance						
Plans	3.0	12.6	23.2	32.4	53.1	70.5
Participants	5.0	13.1	22.5	31.9	52.3	68.3
Number of starts	51	404	508	491	388	550
Services						
Plans	0.0	27.4	28.0	34.7	54.1	72.4
Participants	0.0	28.4	22.8	27.6	49.1	70.4
Number of starts	14	124	414	1,514	1,123	1,219

(Table continues)

TABLE 7–5 (continued)

Industry	Before 1941	1942–1953	1954–1963	1964–1973	1974–1979	1980–1985
Plans	10.4	16.8	24.8	31.3	47.4	60.0
Participants	13.7	18.1	24.9	29.9	46.3	57.2
Number of starts	212	2,214	4,747	8,571	5,628	5,849
Total						

a. The percentage of all primary plans started during the period that were defined contribution.
b. The percentage of all participants in primary plans started during the period that were in defined contribution plans.
c. The number of plans that were started during the period that are still operating in 1985.
SOURCE: 5500 Reporting Forms, 1985.

half of the participants in plans started during this period. As with the smaller plans, the trend toward greater use of defined contribution plans is apparent in virtually all industries.

Summary of Post-ERISA Period

The primary objectives of federal pension policy beginning with ERISA have been to (1) decrease the pension loss associated with job changes, (2) ensure that funding is adequate, (3) ensure that workers receive sufficient information to evaluate their plan, and (4) provide for new types of tax qualified defined contribution plans. Considerable strides have been made toward achieving each of these objectives; however, there apparently has been an unintended side effect of these regulations. The evolving federal regulation has raised the cost of offering all forms of pensions, but it has come down heaviest on defined benefit plans. In response, many firms and workers have shifted from negotiating defined benefit plans to defined contribution plans. In addition, the total pension coverage rate may have been adversely affected.

Firms and workers are increasingly choosing to adopt defined contribution plans instead of defined benefit plans as the primary method of providing retirement income. Defined contribution plans are being used more and more in all industries and for all plan sizes. The trend toward greater use of defined contribution plans is evident from both the number of plans or the number of participants covered by these plans.

The trend away from defined benefit plans has been widespread

TABLE 7–6

New Plans in Firms with 1,000 or More Employees That Were
Defined Contribution Plans, by Industry, from before 1941 to
1985
(percent)

Industry	Before 1941	1942– 1953	1954– 1963	1964– 1973	1974– 1979	1980– 1985
Agriculture						
Plan[a]	0.0	0.0	0.0	27.3	50.0	50.0
Participants[b]	0.0	0.0	0.0	30.9	53.6	73.0
Number of starts[c]	0	7	12	11	12.0	6.0
Mining						
Plan	0.0	8.3	21.4	5.9	13.3	36.8
Participants	0.0	22.7	4.4	7.6	3.1	68.1
Number of starts	3	24	14	17	15	19
Construction						
Plan	50.0	3.6	4.1	22.4	68.4	88.8
Participants	18.9	0.4	6.0	19.1	77.1	91.6
Number of starts	2	28	193	205	57	89
Manufacturing						
Plan	2.6	5.7	9.2	11.9	27.2	37.1
Participants	0.3	2.6	7.3	9.7	19.5	46.6
Number of starts	114	595	556	561	283	337
Transportation						
Plan	1.9	0.0	3.1	13.9	54.2	30.4
Participants	1.4	0.0	9.0	8.3	60.6	13.0
Number of starts	54	99	129	79	59	79
Wholesale trade						
Plan	33.3	25.0	11.6	26.9	35.7	50.0
Participants	39.5	7.7	10.1	21.9	37.5	45.5
Number of starts	3	20	43	52	28	16
Retail trade						
Plan	40.0	24.5	25.0	29.8	30.5	72.5
Participants	1.9	17.0	12.4	23.5	40.4	61.2
Number of starts	5	49	80	168	95	69
Finance						
Plan	1.7	5.4	13.2	20.3	37.0	47.5
Participants	0.3	8.4	5.6	15.7	47.2	40.9
Number of starts	59	202	106	118	73	101
Services						
Plan	0.0	15.2	7.7	8.6	30.5	56.8
Participants	0.0	4.8	6.8	9.3	30.5	74.0
Number of starts	7	66	246	431	164	111

(Table continues)

89

TABLE 7-6 (continued)

Industry	Before 1941	1942–1953	1954–1963	1964–1973	1974–1979	1980–1985
Plan	3.6	6.9	9.0	15.4	34.6	49.2
Participants	0.9	4.6	7.8	14.4	34.9	45.3
Number of starts	247	1090	1379	1642	786	827
Total						

a. The percentage of all primary plans started during the period that were defined contribution.
b. The percentage of all participants in primary plans started during the period that were in defined contribution plans.
c. The number of plans that were started during the period that are still operating in 1985.
Source: 5500 Reporting Forms, 1985.

and has coincided with increased government regulation of the pension contract. This does not prove that the regulatory initiatives caused the decline in the use of defined benefit plans. At least two other factors could have contributed to the changes we observe in the pension universe. First, structural changes in the composition of the economy and labor force may account for some of the increased reliance on defined contribution plans. This would follow from the decline in unionism, reduced employment in the manufacturing sector, and increased employment in the services.

Second, there may have been changes in the degree of risk associated with each type of plan. If these risk factors have indeed changed during the past fifteen years, they may also help to explain the increased reliance on defined contribution plans.

8
Explaining the Trend toward Defined Contribution Plans

The large and widespread shift toward greater use of defined contribution plans and the decreased reliance on defined benefit plans in
recent years can be attributed to a number of factors. The evidence
strongly indicates that changes in the composition of the work force
and structural shifts in the economy account for only a small part of
the shift. Although we are unable to formally test for the impact of
changes in risk during this period, we believe that these changes, too,
had only a small influence on the trend away from defined benefit
plans. Our statistical analysis indicates that the primary cause of this
trend is the change in the regulatory environment. We proceed by
first assessing the impact of structural changes on pension demand
using data from the May 1983 Current Population Survey (CPS)
and the Survey of Consumer Finances (SCF). Next, we use data from
the 5500 reporting forms and the CPS from 1977 to 1985 to test the
effects of changes in industrial composition and other important shifts
in the economy on the types of plans offered by firms.

Pension Coverage and Plan Choice—Analysis of CPS and SCF Data

A firm's decision to offer pension coverage depends on the net cost of
providing the pension. A worker's decision to accept a job with a
pension depends on the net expected value of the job compared with
that of other jobs that do not include pensions as part of their compensation package. The preceding chapters have described the value of
pensions to workers and firms and indicated how this value differs
between defined benefit plans and defined contribution plans. These
concepts are now related to an empirical model of pension coverage
and plan choice.[1] The dependent variables are coverage by any pension plan in the coverage equation and coverage by a defined benefit
plan in the plan choice equation. The independent variables in the
analysis are a series of economic and demographic variables that
explain the decision to accept pension coverage or the choice of a plan

type. Some of the explanatory variables (industry, occupation, union, and others) are dichotomous (0, 1). They indicate whether the observation has this characteristic or not. Results are reported for pension coverage equations estimated from the 1979 and 1983 CPS pension supplements. Also reported are estimates for a pension coverage equation and plan choice equation obtained from the 1983 SCF. The variable means are reported in appendix A along with pension coverage rates in these surveys. The findings are examined for implications concerning changes in pension coverage and plan choice between 1979 and 1983.

Empirical Model of Pension Coverage and Plan Choice. The decision to offer or to accept a pension plan depends, among other things, on the tax advantages that pension coverage provides. Workers and firms facing high tax rates will both benefit from having pensions. Because of the progressive income tax, workers with higher earnings will benefit more in relation to workers with lower earnings from the tax advantages of pension coverage. The relationship between earnings and the type of pension chosen is less certain. Thus, we expect that earnings will be positively associated with pension coverage but have no specific prediction concerning the relationship between earnings and the probability of a pension participant being covered by a defined benefit plan.

As mentioned earlier, a distinctive feature of defined benefit plans is that they can be used as part of implicit employment contracts to modify worker behavior by giving them an incentive not to quit and not to engage in activities that could lead to their dismissal. Firms in which high training costs are associated with firm-specific human capital will be more likely to select defined benefit plans so they can reduce their turnover rates. Firms with high hiring and high monitoring costs will also tend to offer pensions and choose defined benefit plans. To capture some of the variation in these effects across the economy, we include industry dichotomous variables and indicator variables for the occupation of the worker in our equations for both pension coverage and plan choice.

In general, larger plans offer some economies of administration.[2] In addition, some of the regulatory costs per participant decline with large plan size. Thus, the relative costs of offering a defined benefit plan will fall as the number of participants increases. Therefore, larger firms are more likely to offer a pension, and the pension is more likely to be a defined benefit plan. Conversely, workers in larger firms have more opportunity for job advancement and diversification than similar workers in smaller firms. Therefore workers should be less likely to quit and more likely to demand defined benefit plans because of the reduced labor market risks.

Those who are union members have an organization working on their behalf to monitor firm compliance with any implicit contract. As a result, the employer will be discouraged from reneging on the pension contract by terminating the plan or laying off senior workers. In turn, workers will be more willing to accept a pension and the pension is more likely to be a defined benefit plan. Since perceived labor market risk and financial market risk may vary by individual characteristics, we include a series of demographic variables in the pension coverage equations.

Determinants of Pension Coverage. We estimated pension coverage equations for full-time workers in each of the three surveys we examined. Mean coverage rates and sample means for the three samples are shown in appendix tables A–1 and A–2. The samples used in the estimation differ somewhat from those used to determine the means because values are missing for some of the explanatory variables. The dependent variable in these equations is equal to one if the worker is covered by a pension and zero otherwise. The primary result of the loss in observations is the higher pension coverage rate for the 1979 CPS estimating sample.

The results from estimating these equations, shown in table 8–1, are consistent with the predictions of an economic model of pension coverage. The values in the table represent the change in the predicted probability evaluated at the sample means of a worker being covered by a pension for a one-unit change in the explanatory variable.[3] For example, the values in the pension coverage equations shown in table 8–1 for males are -0.022 to -0.026. Thus, if all other factors are held constant, males are 2 to 3 percent less likely to be covered by a pension than females.

Workers in larger firms are much more likely to be covered by pensions than those in smaller firms. The two CPS equations indicate that workers in firms with fewer than 100 employees are more than 30 percent less likely to have pensions than workers in firms with more than 1,000 employees. Workers in firms with 100 to 999 employees are 9 to 17 percent less likely to have pensions. The SCF indicates only whether a worker is employed with a firm that has more or fewer than 100 employees. Estimates for this size variable suggest that workers in firms with fewer than 100 workers are about one-third less likely to be covered by a pension.

Another finding shows that union members are 19 to 30 percent more likely to be covered by a pension than nonunion members and that an extra year of job tenure increases the probability of being covered by a pension. The CPS estimates indicate that a $1 per hour higher wage rate increases the probability of pension coverage by 6 to 8 percent. Surprisingly, the wage effect is zero in the SCF estimates. In these equations, the wage effect is reduced by inclusions of other variables such as education and tenure, which are positively correlated with hourly wage rate.

The education variables indicate that increased educational attainment is associated with a greater likelihood of being covered by a pension. In general, the other demographic variables are not statistically significant from zero. The industrial variables indicate that workers in the agricultural, construction, transportation, retail trade, and service sectors are less likely to be covered than are manufacturing workers.

These estimates allow us to predict what the percentage of pension coverage in the labor force would be if we knew its industrial composition and worker characteristics. If the CPS sample means are used to describe the 1979 and 1983 labor force the percentage of the work force covered by a pension is predicted to drop from 63.7 percent in 1979 to 55.0 percent in 1983. The decline in pension coverage of 8.7 percentage points in the likelihood of being covered by a pension can be decomposed into a reduction in the incidence of pension coverage due to compositional changes in the economy and a decline due to the pension coverage decision process.

Evaluating the estimated 1979 probit function using the 1983 mean values of the explanatory variables predicts the percentage of pension coverage that would have occurred as a result of structural changes in the economy and labor force. This process holds the pension coverage decision constant in its 1979 form as estimated by the 1979 coverage equation. In response to compositional changes in the economy between 1979 and 1983, the pension coverage rate would decline to 56.2 percent. Thus, changes in the economic and demographic variables account for 7.5 percentage points of the observed 8.7 percentage point decline in predicted coverage. Most of the observed decline in pension coverage between 1979 and 1983 was therefore due to changes in the economy and not to the value or cost of pensions.

Determinants of Plan Choice. Heads of households in the SCF were asked a number of questions about their pensions, and the employers of these workers were asked to provide detailed plan characteristics.[4] We use the employer-provided pension data to determine if the respondent is covered by a defined benefit plan, a defined contribution plan, or both. If the respondent is covered by both plan types, he or she is considered to have defined benefit coverage. Estimates of the plan choice equation using the 1983 SCF are shown in column 4 of table 8–1. The dependent variable in these equations is equal to one if the worker is covered by any defined benefit plan. The explanatory variables are the same as those used in the pension coverage equation.

These results are consistent with the economic model of the choice of plan type. First, workers in firms with fewer than 100 employees are 15.2 percent less likely to be covered by a defined benefit plan than workers in larger firms. Union members are 8.4 percent more likely to be covered by a defined benefit plan, and each additional year of tenure is associated with a 0.3 higher probability of being in a defined benefit plan. Controlling for these economic and demographic variables, workers in construction are less likely to be in defined benefit plans, and transportation workers are more likely to be in defined benefit plans than similar workers in manufacturing. No other demographic or economic variables are statistically significant. The predicted percentage at the sample means of defined benefit coverage in this survey is 92.0 percent.

Since there are no time-series data on individual pension coverage by plan type, we are unable to compare plan-choice equations directly at various times to determine the extent to which changes in the choice equation versus changes in the economic and demographic variables explain the trend toward greater use of defined contribution plans. The CPS data can be used to provide some indirect evidence on this question. To this end, we use the 1983 SCF estimates of the plan-choice equations to predict the proportion of pension participants covered by defined benefit plans in the 1979 and 1983 CPS samples.

The 1979 and 1983 CPS means are used with the SCF plan-choice equation to predict the probability of being covered by a defined benefit plan in the respective years under consideration. This assumes that the process by which a plan type is chosen is the same across the two CPS samples and that this process is correctly estimated using the SCF sample. According to the SCF equation, defined benefit coverage was 87.4 percent of pension participants in the 1979 CPS sample and 87.3 percent in the 1983 CPS sample. This small change represents the decline in the defined benefit coverage rate that would have occurred because of changes in the economic and demographic variables that determine plan choice. However, we know that the incidence of defined benefit coverage actually fell substantially during this period. Therefore, these results are evidence that the observed decline in the rate of defined benefit coverage is due to

TABLE 8–1

ESTIMATED PENSION COVERAGE PROBIT FUNCTIONS, 1979 AND 1983

Variable	Pension Coverage			Defined Benefit Coverage
	1979 CPS	1983 CPS	1983 SCF	1983 SCF
Age	0.002[a]	−0.001[b]	0.000	−0.001
Nonwhite	−0.020	0.003	−0.039	0.047
Male	−0.026	−0.026[b]	−0.022	0.016
Education				
12–15 years	0.045[c]	0.058[a]	0.125[a]	0.021
16 or more	0.036	0.075[a]	0.022[a]	−0.002
Married	0.048[a]	0.046[c]	0.048	−0.035
Employer size				
Less than 25	−0.495[a]	−0.456[a]		
25–99	−0.331[a]	−0.299[a]		
100–499	−0.165[a]	−0.168[a]		
500–999	−0.085[a]	−0.098[a]		
Less than 100			−0.345[a]	−0.152[a]
Industry				
Agriculture	−0.176[c]	−0.167[a]	−0.456[a]	0.081
Mining	−0.055	0.010	0.118	0.070
Construction	−0.230[a]	−0.213[a]	−0.198[a]	−0.145[c]
Transportation	−0.205[a]	−0.113[a]	−0.096[b]	0.086[c]
Wholesale trade	−0.023	0.033	−0.015[c]	−0.022
Retail trade	0.134[a]	−0.133[a]	−0.177[a]	−0.087
Finance	−0.011	0.045[c]	−0.046	−0.025
Services	−0.109[a]	−0.088[a]	−0.161[a]	−0.019
Occupation				
Professional	0.038[a]	0.006	0.098[c]	0.011
Clerical	0.097[a]	0.058[a]	0.035	0.035
Union	0.187[a]	0.186[a]	0.299[a]	0.084[a]
Wage	0.080[a]	0.060[a]	0.000	0.000
Tenure	0.004[a]	0.019[a]	0.012[a]	0.003[c]
Constant	−0.333[a]	−0.355[a]	−0.076	0.155
Proportion covered	0.600	0.528	0.623	0.878
Predicted probability	0.637	0.550	0.658	0.920
Log of likelihood function	−4,592	−5,457	−663	−176

a. Estimated coefficients are significantly different from zero at the .01 confidence level.

b. Estimated coefficients are significantly different from zero at the .05 confidence level.

c. Estimated coefficients are significantly different from zero at the .10 confidence level.

SOURCE: 1979 and 1983 May Supplement, Current Population Survey, and 1983 Survey of Consumer Finances.

changes in the plan choice decision itself, and not to demographic changes in the labor force or structural changes in the economy.

Estimates of Plan Choice Using Firm Data

Data from the 5500 reporting forms and CPS can be used to study how changes in industrial composition and other important shifts in the economy affect the decisions of firms to offer defined benefit plans. Here we use data from 1977 (the first year in which data from 5500 reporting forms appear on computer files) and 1985 (the last currently available reporting year on data tapes), as well as worker characteristics from the 1977 and 1985 CPS data.

Pensions are limited to primary plans as determined by the Department of Labor,[5] and the sample is further restricted to single-employer plans with 100 or more participants. Firms are grouped according to whether they offer at least one primary defined benefit plan or whether none of their primary pension plans are defined benefit plans. Thus, if a firm has both a primary defined benefit plan covering some workers and another primary defined contribution plan covering other workers, the firm is characterized as providing defined benefit coverage. In effect, the analysis is biased toward indicating greater defined benefit coverage.

Other information used from the 5500 reporting form data includes the number of employees, the effective date of the oldest plan, and the industry of the firm. Because the 5500 reporting form data contain no information on worker characteristics, sample means for age, education, and hourly wage for ninety-five detailed industry groupings were obtained from the 1977 and 1985 CPS surveys. The percentages of nonwhite workers, male workers, married workers, union workers, and three occupational groupings for the same ninety-five industry groupings also come from the CPS.

Analysis of 5500 Data. Sample means and percentages for the samples used in the analysis are reported in table 8–2, which shows the mean values for the dependent variable (defined benefit plans) and all the explanatory variables used in the analysis. All except the demographic variables are dichotomous (0,1) so that the values shown in the table represent the proportion of sample observations with this attribute. For example, in 1977, 51.5 percent of all firms with primary pension plans with 100 or more participants had between 100 and 499 employees. The demographic variables are obtained from the CPS and are the mean values from the survey.

These data show the structural changes in the economy between 1977 and 1985. Firms with fewer than 500 employees offering pension

TABLE 8–2

SAMPLE MEANS FOR 5500 TAX REPORTING FORMS AND CPS,
1977 AND 1985

	1977		1985	
	5500 Forms	CPS	5500 Forms	CPS
Defined benefit plans	0.699		0.561	
Number of employees				
100–499	0.515		0.557	
500–999	0.179		0.160	
More than 1,000	0.306		0.283	
Effective date				
Before 1942	0.030		0.016	
1942–1953	0.170		0.103	
1954–1963	0.251		0.168	
1964–1973	0.383		0.302	
1974–1979	0.167		0.206	
1980–1985			0.206	
Industry				
Agriculture	0.008	0.042	0.010	0.034
Mining	0.019	0.011	0.021	0.012
Construction	0.020	0.072	0.025	0.077
Manufacturing	0.462	0.281	0.424	0.238
Transportation	0.064	0.074	0.051	0.084
Wholesale trade	0.064	0.050	0.070	0.047
Retail trade	0.068	0.140	0.079	0.141
Finance	0.135	0.062	0.118	0.073
Services	0.160	0.269	0.203	0.294
Demographics				
Age		38.26		37.73
Nonwhite		0.107		0.125
Male		0.647		0.614
Married		0.724		0.669
Education		13.34		13.93
Professional workers		0.241		0.258
Technical, clerical		0.283		0.386
Production workers		0.476		0.356
Union		0.265		0.204
Wage (1977 dollars)		4.733		5.163
Sample size	13,692	48,119	25,709	51,831

SOURCE: 5500 Tax Reporting Forms, 1977 and 1985.

plans increased in relation to those with 500 or more employees. Decreased employment in the manufacturing sector and increased employment in the service sector account for the largest changes in industrial composition. The demographic composition of the work force also changed. The percentage of male workers and married workers declined, whereas the percentage of nonwhite workers increased. The occupational mix was altered as a result of decreased employment among production workers and increased employment among technical workers. Unionism declined about 6 percent and real wages rose 0.9 percent.

The change between 1977 and 1985 in the percentages of firms offering at least one defined benefit plan for the nine one-digit industries is shown in table 8–3. Across all industries, the percentage of firms offering defined benefit plans declined 13.4 percent, and declines were observed in all nine of the major industry categories. The largest decline (19.6 percent) occurred in the service sector, and the smallest decline (8.7 percent) occurred in the wholesale trade industry. Considering all of the ninety-five detailed industry categories, the percentage of firms offering defined benefit plans declined in all but four of these industries with 63 percent of the declines statistically significant at the .10 level of significance. Of the four industries in which the number of firms offering defined benefit plans actually increased, none are statistically significant. These results are shown in appendix table B–1.

Total employment declined in thirty-two of the ninety-five industries, and the percentage of firms offering defined benefit plans in these declining industries fell by 11 percent compared with 14.3 percent in those industries in which employment increased. The percentage of unionized workers increased in only eleven of the ninety-five industries, but even in these industries the percentage of firms offering defined benefit plans declined. The decline of 13.6 percent in industries where unionism increased is not statistically different from the 13.3 percent decline observed in those industries in which unionization decreased. In the eighty-one industries in which the percentage of production workers decreased, the percentage of firms offering defined benefit plans declined 13.7 percent, in comparison with a 10.7 percent decline in those industries in which the employment of these workers increased. These comparisons further illustrate the broad decline in the use of defined benefit plans.

Plan-Choice Functions. The choice of pension plan type is estimated using the data from the 5500 reporting forms. The dependent variable is equal to one if the firm offers at least one primary defined benefit

TABLE 8–3
Changes in Defined Benefit Coverage, by Industry, 1977–1985

Industry	Percentage Change[a]
All industries	− 13.4
Agriculture, forestry, and fisheries	− 17.2
Mining	− 18.8
Construction	− 17.1
Manufacturing	− 10.6
Transportation, communications, and other public utilities	− 13.7
Wholesale trade	− 8.7
Retail trade	− 11.4
Finance, insurance, and real estate	− 10.9
Services	− 19.6

a. All changes are significantly different from zero at the .01 confidence level.
Source: 5500 Tax Reporting Forms, 1977 and 1985.

plan and zero otherwise. The results shown in table 8–4 indicate the change in the predicted probability of a firm offering a defined benefit plan if the explanatory variable changes in value from zero to one, or by one unit. The base case against which these effects are calculated is a manufacturing firm with more than 1,000 workers, whose oldest plan was started between 1964 and 1973. The estimates shown in the first and third columns of table 8–4 include the CPS means for the 95 industry groupings. The estimates shown in the second and fourth columns do not include the data from the CPS but do include dichotomous variables for 110 industry groupings.

The 1977 estimates indicate that firms with 100 to 499 employees were 18 percent less likely to offer a defined benefit plan, while firms with 500 to 999 were 11 percent less likely to offer a defined benefit plan than firms with more than 1,000 workers. The industry variables predict that after controlling for size and worker characteristics, firms in all industries except agriculture, construction, and mining are more likely to offer only defined contribution plans than are manufacturing firms. The estimates range from 4.5 to 34.6 percentage points.[6]

The effective date variables provide several interesting results. First, firms whose oldest plan was started prior to 1942 and was still in effect in 1977 are over 20 percent more likely to offer defined benefit plans than are firms whose oldest plan was started between 1964 and 1973. Apparently, there was an early trend toward greater use of defined contribution plans as pension spread throughout the economy up until the mid-1950s. In the two decades prior to ERISA,

TABLE 8–4

ESTIMATED DEFINED BENEFIT COVERAGE, 5500 FORMS, 1977 AND 1985

	1977		1985	
Number of employees				
100–499	−0.181[a]	−0.187[a]	−0.264[a]	−0.251[a]
500–999	−0.107[a]	−0.118[a]	−0.183[a]	−0.180[a]
Effective date				
Before 1942	0.210[a]	0.203[a]	0.236[a]	0.262[a]
1942–1953	0.100[a]	0.092[a]	0.153[a]	0.169[a]
1954–1963	0.010	0.010	0.042[a]	0.049[a]
1974–1979	−0.120[a]	−0.116[a]	−0.163[a]	−0.159[a]
1980–1985			−0.309[a]	−0.302[a]
Industry				
Agriculture	0.162[a]		0.129[a]	
Mining	0.039		−0.012	
Construction	−0.338[a]		−0.300[a]	
Transportation	−0.134[a]		−0.127[a]	
Wholesale trade	−0.176[a]		−0.248[a]	
Retail trade	−0.346[a]		−0.361[a]	
Finance	−0.045		−0.089[a]	
Services	−0.112[a]		−0.137[a]	
Demographics				
Age	0.003		0.004	
Nonwhite	0.004[a]		0.005[a]	
Male	−0.000		−0.001[a]	
Married	−0.003[c]		0.004[a]	
Education	−0.038[a]		−0.035[b]	
Professional workers	0.003[a]		0.001	
Technical, clerical	0.005[a]		0.004[a]	
Union	0.004[a]		0.003[a]	
Wage (1977 dollars)	0.054[a]		0.040[a]	
Constant	0.405[b]	0.249[a]	0.106	0.239[a]
Proportion defined benefit plans	0.697	0.697	0.561	0.561
Predicted probability	0.714	0.728	0.577	0.580
Log likelihood of function	−7,118	−6,901	−13,375	−12,722

NOTE: Equations shown in columns 2 and 4 also included 110 dichotomous variables indicating the three-digit SCC code of the plan sponsor.
a. Estimated coefficients are significantly different from zero at the .01 confidence level.
b. Estimated coefficients are significantly different from zero at the .05 confidence level.
c. Estimated coefficients are significantly different from zero at the .10 confidence level.
SOURCE: 5500 Tax Reporting Forms, 1977 and 1985.

however, there was apparently not much change in the probability of firms offering defined benefit plans. The effective date coefficient for plans begun in 1954 to 1963 shows that firms whose oldest plan was started between 1954 and 1963 are 1 percent more likely to offer defined benefit plans than are firms that started their oldest plan between 1964 and 1973. Thus, during this twenty-year period the choice of plan type seems to have been relatively stable.

After the passage of ERISA in 1974, there is a sharp decline in the probability of pensions being defined benefit plans. The 1977 estimates indicate that firms whose oldest plan was started between 1974 and 1977 were 12 percent less likely to offer defined benefit plans than firms whose oldest plan was started between 1964 and 1973.

The estimates also indicate that a firm's decision to offer or not to offer defined benefit plans is influenced by the demographic characteristics of its work force. Firms in industries with a more educated work force are more likely to offer only defined contribution plans. Higher percentages of professional, technical, and clerical workers relative to production workers and higher wages increase the probability that firms will offer defined benefit plans. A one percentage point decrease in unionism decreases the probability of firms offering defined benefit plans by 0.4 percentage points.

The industry and employer size variables are consistent with the economic model of plan choice outlined throughout this report. The positive effects of unionism and wages are also consistent with labor contracting. Perhaps the most interesting finding from these estimates is the pattern of the coefficients on the effective date of the plan. There is a large jump in the likelihood of firms offering defined contribution plans just after the passage of ERISA, whereas there was no trend toward greater use of defined contribution plans just before 1974.

In general, the 1985 estimates are qualitatively consistent with those in the 1977 equation. The size effects are greater and indicate that firms with 100 to 499 workers are now 25 to 26 percent less likely to offer defined benefit plans and firms with 500 to 999 are 18 percent less likely to offer defined benefit plans than are firms with 1,000 employees. The effective date coefficients reveal that the trend toward greater use of defined contribution plans accelerated during the 1980s. Firms whose oldest plans were started between 1980 and 1985 are 14 percent less likely to offer defined benefit plans than those whose oldest plans were started between 1974 and 1979 and 30 percent more likely to offer defined contribution plans than those started in the decade prior to the passage of ERISA. The industry coefficients indicate that firms in nonmanufacturing industries are increasingly more likely to offer defined contribution plans than are manufacturing firms. There are virtually no differences in the estimated effects of worker characteristics on plan choice.

Comparing the 1985 estimates to those of 1977 provides several interesting observations. First, the increased difference in the probability of smaller firms offering defined contribution plans suggests that changes in the plan choice process have been largest among smaller firms. This is consistent with the finding that regulatory changes raise the price of defined benefit plans and that these effects are larger for smaller firms. We also have estimated plan choice equations separately by firm size. These estimates indicate a decline in the use of defined benefit plans in all size categories, with the largest declines occurring among the smaller plans.

According to the model based only on data from the 5500 forms (columns 2 and 4), 72.8 percent of firms were likely to offer at least one primary defined benefit in 1977, in contrast to 58.0 percent in 1985. This represents a decline in the probability of firms offering defined benefit plans of 14.8 percentage points between 1977 and 1985. Statistical tests confirm that the estimated coefficients of the two equations are significantly different.[7] To evaluate the importance of changes in industrial composition in comparison with changes in the plan choice process, the plan-choice equations for both years are estimated without the effective date variables.[8] According to this estimation, the predicted probability of a firm offering a defined benefit plan is 72.2 percent in 1977 and 57.2 percent in 1985.

The proportion of defined benefit coverage predicted by the estimated 1977 probit function with the 1985 sample means for the explanatory variables is 69.1 percent. In other words, if the plan-choice process remained constant and only the economy changed (as it actually did during this period), 69.1 percent of firms would have offered defined benefit plans in 1985. In contrast, if the choice process is allowed to change in conjunction with the economic change, the predicted percentage of firms offering defined benefit plans drops to 57.2 percent. These results indicate that 3.1 percentage points of the predicted 15 percentage point change is due to changes in the size distribution of firms and the industrial composition of the economy between 1977 and 1985. The remaining 79 percent of the total decline in the incidence of defined benefit plans is due to changes in the plan choice process.

Using the CPS data (columns 1 and 3) to decompose the predicted change in defined benefit coverage between 1977 and 1985 into the predicted change attributable to changes in the economy and the predicted change attributable to changes in the choice process yields similar results. If we allow for changes in the choice process and changes in the economy, the incidence of defined benefit plans is predicted to decline 13.8 percentage points. But when the 1985 means are used in the estimated 1977 probit function, the incidence of defined benefit coverage *increases* 4.6 percentage points. The increase in the proportion of smaller firms is predicted to have caused a slight decrease of 0.6 percent in the incidence of defined benefit plans. Defined benefit coverage is predicted to have declined by 1 percent because of changes in the industrial composition that occurred between 1977 and 1985, and the decline in unionism is predicted to have caused a 2 percent decline. Offsetting these declines is a predicted increase of 5.7 percent caused by the increase in technical and clerical workers relative to production workers and a predicted increase of 2.7 percent caused by the 0.9 percent rise in real wages. The predicted change caused by demographic changes in the work force is negligible.[9]

Why the Plan-Choice Process Has Changed

The evidence presented in the preceding sections strongly suggests that changes in the plan-choice process have produced the decline in defined benefit coverage since 1974. The decision parameters changed in response to increased costs and reduced benefits associated with defined benefit plans. The most likely explanation for these changes and the timing of the effects is the evolving federal regulation of pensions. An alternative explanation is that the magnitude of the risks associated with each plan type may have changed. Earlier we indicated that plan type choice was a function of financial market risks, labor market risks, and inflationary risks. We now examine how these factors have changed during the past twenty years and assess whether changes in these forms of risk may have contributed to the trend toward greater use of defined contribution plans.

In general, participants in defined benefit plans do not bear the risk of short-run variation in the actual rate of return on invested pension funds. Therefore increased volatility in financial markets should increase the demand for defined benefit plans. A recent study of the volatility of asset market returns indicates that bond and stock volatility was high during 1969 to 1971 prior to ERISA and again in 1974 and 1975 immediately after the passage of ERISA.[10] Between 1969 and 1971, defined benefit plans as a percentage of net plans created (new plan formations less plans terminated) increased from 52.3 percent to 56 percent, whereas between 1974 and 1975 the percentage declined from 54.8 percent to 49.1 percent.[11] Examination of the fluctuations in monthly Aaa bond returns since 1857 shows that the most volatile period occurred between 1979 and 1988. Again, despite this increased volatility in the bond market, the percentage of new plans that were defined benefit plans had declined even further to 32.7 percent by 1983.

In the labor market, an increase in the risk of job loss should decrease the demand for defined benefit plans. If the desire for more job mobility increases among workers, the demand for defined benefit plans should also decrease. In the decade preceding ERISA (1964–1973), when the percentage of defined benefit plans was increasing, quit rates rose from 1.3 percent to 2.4 percent. This represented an increase in the quit rate of 61 percent. Layoff rates, on the other hand, fell from 1.5 percent to 0.8 percent. This represents a decline in the layoff rate of 63 percent.[12] Between 1974 and 1979, however, quit rates fell 21 percent and layoff rates fell 41 percent. In the decade before ERISA when the proportion of defined benefit plans was increasing, job losers as a percentage of the work force fluctuated between 1.3 percent and 2.8 percent.[13] After ERISA, job losers fluctuated between 2.4 and 5.7 percent of the labor force. This structural pattern of quit and layoff rates is not consistent evidence that labor market conditions caused the decline in defined benefit plans during the post-ERISA period.

Workers in defined benefit plans also face the risk of firm failure. As this risk increases, so does the probability that workers will not receive their promised benefits at retirement. Furthermore, firms will be less willing to bear the short-run financial risks involved in defined benefit pensions. Therefore increases in firm failure rates should be associated with a reduction in the incidence of defined benefit plans. Between 1964 and 1973, firm failure rates declined 38 percent. This decline continued into the period between 1974 and 1979, when the decline in defined benefit coverage began. During this period, firm failure rates declined 32.3 percent. During the 1980s, however, firm failure rates increased from 42.1 to 102 per 10,000 establishments. This large increase in firm failure rates in the 1980s is consistent with declining defined benefit plans. However, the declining rates between 1974 and 1979 are not consistent with the large drop in defined benefit plans observed during that period.

Firms bear preretirement inflation risks if returns on pension funds do not match price increases. Workers bear postretirement inflation risks, however, if there are no postretirement adjustments in benefits. Therefore the effects of changes in inflation risks on the incidence of defined benefit plans are also ambiguous. During the pre-ERISA period, when the percentage of defined benefit plans was increasing, inflation rates rose steadily, except for a slight decline between 1969 and 1972. The post-ERISA period is characterized by falling inflation rates between 1974 and 1975, followed by the very high rates of inflation during the late 1970s and then declining rates in the 1980s. If inflation risks were associated with the declines in defined benefit coverage during this period, we would expect a similar cyclic pattern in the incidence of defined benefit coverage rather than the steady decline that is observed in the data.

In summary, the risks faced by workers and firms have fluctuated throughout the post-ERISA period. The volatility of inflation rates, firm failure rates, asset yields, and layoff rates all increased during this period. However, none of the changes in these risks are consistent with the steady increase in defined benefit plans before 1974 and the sharp decline after 1974. In response to observed changes in these risk factors, defined benefit coverage should have had periods of increases as well as decreases.

The fact that the use of defined benefit plans continues to decline suggests that fluctuations in risks that influence plan choice have not played an important role in the trend toward defined contribution plans. The long-run trend away from defined benefit plans, however, is consistent with the evolution of federal pension regulation since 1974. Pension regulation appears to be largely responsible for the greater use of defined contribution plans.

9
Prospects for the Future

During the past century, the private pension system in the United States has evolved in response to changing federal policy in conjunction with a maturing economy, rising real incomes, and an aging population. The increased life expectancy and desire for sufficient income to enjoy old age without having to be engaged in full-time work have increased the demand for retirement income. Although federal tax policy and direct government regulation have shaped the structure of the current pension system, a formal system of retirement savings would have emerged without these factors. However, the existence of governmental oversight has played a central role in the development of our current system of employer-provided pensions.

Declining Dominance of Defined Benefit Plans, Key Findings

Prior to 1974, most pension participants were in defined benefit plans. These plans were first introduced during the latter part of the nineteenth century and spread to many large employers between 1900 and 1920. As the nation's pension system continued to evolve, defined benefit plans were usually chosen as the primary retirement plan. This was especially true in large, unionized firms. Although defined benefit plans remained as primary retirement plans, the period between 1940 and 1974 saw an increase in the number of defined contribution plans offered as supplemental plans. As the tax rates rose during and following World War II, the cost of tax-qualified plans decreased. Coverage therefore expanded, and throughout this period plans were modified in accordance with pension standards necessary to achieve favored tax status.[1]

Despite the pre-ERISA dominance of defined benefit plans, many workers and firms chose defined contribution plans for their primary pension coverage. In this unregulated environment, both parties could consider the gains and cost of each type of plan. Although most workers and firms selected defined benefit plans, some found defined contribution plans to be more advantageous. Over time, the proportion of workers and firms deciding that defined contribution plans offer greater value has risen. This change in the choice of a pension has been induced by government regulation.

ERISA and subsequent pension regulations have substantially raised the price of offering defined benefit plans relative to that of defined contribution plans and reduced the gain from using defined benefit plans as part of implicit employment contracts. In particular, the cost has been affected by funding standards, reporting requirements, and the mandatory purchase of insurance. With the institution and subsequent lowering of vesting and participation standards, the relative cost of defined benefit plans has also risen. We have emphasized the role defined benefit pensions play in productivity-enhancing employment contracts. Pension penalties that modify worker behavior are fundamental to these contracts. The flexibility that workers and firms have to negotiate these contracts has been eroded by federal pension regulation over the past fifteen years. This has been one of the main factors contributing to the decline of defined benefit plans. The annual regulatory changes occurring during the 1980s have also required firms to rewrite their plans frequently and to incur the expenses of bringing the plan into compliance with the latest regulations. Unfortunately, federal budget deficits have greatly influenced pension policy, which has resulted in policy initiatives that have reduced the desirability of defined benefit plans.

Another adverse effect of the recent legislation has been to limit the ability of firms and workers to institute pension contracts that alter worker incentives for job turnover and retirement. Vesting and participation changes have lowered the costs of job changes, while continuing wage and service accruals and the elimination of mandatory retirement provisions have reduced incentives for retirement. At the same time, there is greater certainty of retirement income for workers, especially job changers, and the value of continued employment has increased for older workers.

As the net value of employment contracts that include defined benefit plans has fallen, more firms and workers have chosen to adopt defined contribution plans. There is a large and widespread movement toward defined contribution plans as the primary retirement plan. This trend is found in all industries, in firms of all sizes, and across workers of all characteristics. It cannot be explained by compositional changes in the economy or by changes in the labor force. Rather, this trend is the result of fundamental changes in the choice of pensions. The principal cause of these changes appears to be the evolving regulatory environment. Apparently, this shift has been an unintended by-product of regulation and has not occurred because of any specific governmental effort to reduce reliance on defined benefit plans.

Future Regulatory Initiatives

Much of the recent pension legislation has been aimed at further reducing the pension cost of changing jobs, reducing retirement incentives, and increasing the security of pension funds. Are past changes in these areas predictors of further regulatory change?

Reduce or Eliminate the Pension Cost of Changing Jobs. The pension cost of leaving a job and the related reduction in turnover has become a topic of public debate. Some analysts are concerned that there is too little mobility among workers in the United States. The characteristics of defined benefit plans that produce a loss in pension wealth with job changes could be further constrained to eliminate this pension loss. For example, firms could be required to offer immediate participation and vesting to all workers. Legislation passed in 1986 lowers the maximum vesting standard to five-year, 100 percent vesting, or graded vesting beginning after three years. Immediate vesting would have only a minor effect on the lifetime pension wealth of a job changer. Therefore, any further reductions in permissible vesting standards will have only limited influence on the job change decisions of most pension participants.

In defined benefit plans with final earnings formulas, the lack of portability of service credits can result in a pension loss for workers who change jobs. To date there has been no legislation mandating portability of accrued service credits across employers. Portability of service credits that would eliminate all pension loss associated with job changes would be extremely difficult to achieve. First, pensions in the United States are quite diverse, so that it would be difficult to match credits across different plans. A new government agency would probably have to be set up to carry out such a task, and its regulatory costs could be quite high.

Second, someone must pay for the added cost to provide the increased benefits to the job changer. The loss in lifetime pension benefits associated with job changing follows from the implicit contract associated with defined benefit plans, which impose costs on workers who violate the contract. The difference between the stay pension and the leave pension described in chapter 4 represents the added costs associated with mandatory portability. Even if firms freely traded assets based on the vested benefits of workers switching jobs, these funds would not be sufficient to pay mobile workers benefits equal to those of single-employer workers. Instead, traded funds would have to be equivalent to the projected benefits based on the implicit contracts that departing workers violated.

Before the benefits of mobile workers can equal those of the single-job workers, either new employers must incur higher costs for new employees who have been covered by pensions or former employers must make additional contributions into the pension accounts of departing workers. Who should be liable for these additional pension costs? Should it be the firms that the workers leave? This would raise the cost of employee turnover to firms and eliminate their ability to use pensions to reduce turnover, and thus make defined benefit pensions less desirable from their viewpoint.

Should new employers be required to make up the differences in pension benefits? Requiring hiring firms to incur additional pension costs at the time of employment will reduce the demand for workers previously covered by pensions. In this case, older workers are the ones most likely to be adversely affected. It should also be remembered that added pension costs placed on firms by federal regulations will likely be passed on to workers as a group in the form of lower wages.

There are several other methods of reducing the loss in pension wealth associated with job changes. First, firms could be required to provide lump-sum distributions to departing workers. If these funds are based on legally vested pension wealth, the average worker will not gain from lump-sum distributions. If the distributions are based on pension wealth using projected future earnings, the pension loss from job changes could be eliminated. This is similar to changing the vesting laws so that workers vest projected benefits on the basis of expected final earnings rather than benefits based on earnings to date. Second, firms could be required to index vested benefits to the average rate of growth of the wages of their employees. Under such a policy, the vested benefit left behind would increase and the real value of the benefits would be maintained.

Both of these methods would substantially reduce and, under certain conditions, eliminate the loss in pension wealth associated with job changes. These types of modifications are examples of how losses could be eliminated without developing a large new, administrative bureaucracy. However, each of these methods as well as portable service credits demonstrates that the primary issues are added costs and the nature of the employment contracts. We would expect higher pension costs to be borne by workers in the form of lower wages. The actual income transfer from this policy will likely be from workers who honor the implicit contract (single-job workers) to workers who violate it (mobile workers).

Since the early 1970s, several proposals have been put forth for increasing the "portability" of pension benefits. These include recommendations by the 1965 Committee on Corporate Pension Funds and Other Private Retirement and Welfare Programs, congressional proposals made during the 1973–1974 ERISA debates, and the recommendation by the Presidential Commission on Pension Policy that a minimum universal pension system be introduced.[2] More recent proposals include the Pension Portability Açt of 1987 and the recommendation of a portable pension plan.[3]

Although many of these proposals use the phrase "portability of pension benefits," their objectives are limited to providing access to the wealth value of vested benefits. They do not specify that service credits should be portable. Instead, they recommend that firms provide lump-sum distributions of vested benefits to terminated employees. Workers could then invest these funds in another form of retirement plan or IRA. Several of these proposals have suggested that the federal government should establish a portability agency or a central clearinghouse for these funds.[4] This would allow job changers to consolidate all pension funds in one agency.

Some of these proposals have also recommended that firms be required to establish defined contribution plans and that a federally administered agency be created to invest these funds and to follow workers from job to job. Such actions might increase pension coverage, but would they increase the pension wealth of persons already covered by a defined benefit pension? The answer seems to be no; they would not provide portability of service credits, and hence they would not reduce the pension loss associated with job changes.

If firms offered cash-outs of vested benefits, workers changing jobs would have greater access to pension funds. A policy of mandatory lump-sum distributions could be easily implemented, but would it increase workers' total retirement benefits? Most workers will not gain from lump-sum distributions, and only persons who accept a high level of risk in investments will be able to improve pension wealth to any degree. A high level of investment risk also can lead to a loss of pension wealth. The greater the risk investors are willing to accept, the greater the opportunity for gains and losses.

Proposals that call for lump-sum distributions will actually do little to counter the losses of pension wealth associated with job changes for workers covered by defined benefit plans. Although these proposals do provide for greater cash-out opportunities and may increase pension coverage, on average, they will have only a

111

small impact on pension wealth at retirement for participants in defined benefit plans. To the extent that these and other proposals are aimed at increasing mobility by reducing the loss of pension wealth associated with job changes, they are not likely to succeed.

If service credits were made portable, administrative costs would increase sharply. Proposals requiring firms to pay benefits based on projected final earnings or to increase vested benefits with increases in average payroll could also substantially reduce losses in pension wealth associated with job changes. Such regulations would tend to increase worker mobility while increasing pension wealth. However, someone would have to bear the added costs—either firms would have to accept lower profits, workers lower wages, or consumers higher prices.

Additional regulations limiting the pension cost of changing jobs will further limit the ability of workers and firms to negotiate long-term employment contracts that include defined benefit plans as the enforcement mechanism. For example, portable service credits would eliminate the central feature of defined benefit plans, their ability to modify worker behavior. Such action would prevent firms and workers from benefiting from lower turnover, reduce investment in human capital, and reduce lifetime compensation for workers. Any future regulatory initiatives in these areas will accelerate the decline of defined benefit plans.

Reduce Retirement Incentives. Firms now are required to continue to credit wage and service accruals as long as workers remain with a firm. This requirement, adopted in 1986, substantially increases the gain from continued employment by increasing pension compensation. Even so, most workers still face a large drop in pension compensation when they reach the age of eligibility for retirement benefits. In most plans, workers who remain on the job past the age of normal retirement do not receive a pension benefit for that year. Moreover, their pensions are not adjusted to the shorter retirement period caused by postponing retirement.

These effects could be eliminated if firms were required to provide actuarial adjustments for delayed retirement or if pensions had to be paid at the normal retirement age, whether the individual retired or remained on the job. Thus, pension compensation would not drop at the age of eligibility and retirement incentives would not gain strength after the normal age of retirement. Consistent with these changes, plans with early retirement options could be required to include actuarial penalties relative to the normal retirement age.

This change would sharply reduce early retirement incentives inherent in most defined benefit plans. Similarly, maximum benefit provisions could be eliminated.

All of these proposals would directly affect another feature of defined benefit plans used to alter worker behavior. By sharply reducing pension compensation at specified ages, defined benefit plans enable firms to incorporate retirement incentives into their compensation system. For firms seeking to set an end point to the employment contract, these incentives are a crucial component of the long-term contract. If they were eliminated, there would be further cause for a decline in the use of defined benefit plans.

Regulate Pension Terminations for Reversion of Assets. Changes in the implied ownership of pension funds would directly affect the desirability of defined benefit plans to workers and firms. Recent proposals by Sen. Howard Metzenbaum and Rep. Howard Clay attempt to restrict the ability of firms to terminate plans to recover excess assets in the plans. The reversion of excess assets to firms is based on the premise that firms are liable for the payment of promised pension benefits. If the employer has contributed too little to the pension fund, contributions must be increased. If the plan is overfunded and the company "owns" the pension fund, then the firm has the right to recover these funds. Currently, the only method of recovering the excess funds is to terminate the existing pension plan and settle all legal claims. This is typically done by buying workers' and retirees' annuities equal to their current or promised pension benefits. Of course, the firm must treat these funds as income for tax purposes and since 1988 must pay a 15 percent surtax on all such funds.

The current system is consistent with the concept that firms own the pension plan and bear the financial risks associated with funding the plan. The firm loses when returns on invested assets are below the expected rate and gains when returns exceed the expected rate. Proposals to restrict reversions seek to change this concept and to make ownership asymmetric; firms still lose with below-expected returns and must increase contributions, but their ability to gain from above-expected returns is limited. Contributions can still be reduced when the fund is performing well, but the firm can no longer gain access to these funds through a reversion.

Retirees often suffer wealth losses when pension plans are terminated, even though firms must pay all promised benefits. Persons already retired lose because their pensions are converted from the company plan to an annuity often paid by an insurance company. Many on-going pension plans provide retirees with periodic increases in benefits to compensate for inflation. The conversion of the pension benefit into an annuity paid by a third party typically results in no further increases in the pension benefit.

Workers can also lose because the terminated plan pays a benefit based on employment to date or a legal pension benefit. If workers have been paying for a projected benefit based on expected earnings at retirement, they suffer a loss in pension wealth just as if they had quit an on-going pension plan (see chapters 4 and 5). This loss can be eliminated if the company starts a new defined benefit plan and gives the worker credit for past service; however, if no new plan is introduced or if the company switches to a defined contribution plan, current workers suffer a real loss in pension wealth.

These losses to retirees and workers can be reduced if the terminating plans are required to settle accounts on the basis of projected benefits or provide for benefits to reflect past inflation. Such requirements are consistent with requiring sponsoring firms to honor implicit, instead of explicit, pension contracts.

Public policy on this issue has become closely intertwined with concerns over the recent pattern of leveraged buyouts. In some cases, acquiring firms have used excess funds in pension plans to finance the acquisition. Management of these new firms is less likely to honor the implicit contract with workers and is thus more likely to terminate the pension plan providing only legally required benefits. Given the termination of existing defined benefit plans, these acquiring firms may now decide to offer only defined contribution plans. In this regard, reducing terminations for reversions may slow the shift toward defined contribution plans.

Policy on plan termination is also closely linked to current budgetary policy. Efforts to raise revenues may be one factor in the imposition of tax penalties on excess funds recovered by the firm.

The important economic questions involved in the rules for termination for reversions are who owns the pension funds, who bears the investment risks, and what the nature of the pension contract is. A comprehensive assessment of the termination-for-reversion issue is beyond the scope of this analysis. Policy makers, however, should consider the impact of any changes in this area on the overall desirability of defined benefit pension plans. New regulatory initiatives are likely to increase the pension wealth of persons now covered by defined benefit plans but reduce the probability that future workers will be covered by defined benefit plans.

Reversing the Trend toward Defined Contribution Plans

We believe that the unmistakable shift in the choice of pensions in recent years—from defined benefit plans toward defined contribution plans—is the response of workers and firms to a changing regulatory environment, in which the net benefit of defined benefit plans has declined. To the extent that defined benefit plans were components of productivity-enhancing employment contracts, the decline in the use of these plans will have an adverse effect on social welfare.

Although 5500 information is only available up to 1985, the changes in pension regulation from 1985 to 1988 lead us to predict that defined benefit plans will be used even less in the near future. Preliminary data from the 1988 EBS seem to confirm this prediction, in that defined benefit coverage among a group of surveyed firms fell from 76 percent of full-time workers in 1986 to 70 percent of workers in 1988.[5]

Beginning with the passage of ERISA, Congress has expanded pension regulation to ensure that defined benefit participants would receive their retirement benefits. In doing so, it did not give sufficient consideration to the impact of these regulations on the choice of a pension. As a result, pension regulation and tax policies in the 1980s have also sparked a sharp decline in the use of defined benefit plans. Some new proposals are currently being debated, but, as already mentioned, they would lead to a further reduction in defined benefit coverage. If policy makers believe that defined benefit plans are desirable, they must consider the possible impact of all future pension regulation on the plan-choice process itself; government regulation cannot be directed solely to the operation of plans, without regard for the impact of these regulations on plan formation.

Can the trend toward greater use of defined contribution plans be reversed by returning federal pension policy to a more neutral position in the plan choice process? A comprehensive deregulation of pensions and a return to pre-ERISA standards is highly unlikely. Once property rights have been established through reduced vesting and participation standards, they are very difficult to repeal. The fact is that some aspects of these regulations have proven highly popular with pension participants in general. Of course, current participants are not the only interested parties; public policy should also be considering the welfare of potential pension participants.

If deregulation is unlikely, what can be done to increase the use of defined benefit plans? First, the government should attempt to achieve some stability in its pension policy. Since the mid-1980s,

115

pension regulations have changed every year. During this period, the cost of operating pension plans has increased substantially as sponsors have found it necessary to modify their plans to conform to the continually changing governmental policies. Short-run federal, budgetary considerations should not be allowed to interfere with the determination of a rational pension policy.

Second, a detailed review of existing pension policies should be conducted to determine where excessive regulatory costs are currently being imposed on defined benefit plans. For example, greater reliance on experience rating for PBGC premiums would lower the administrative costs of adequately funded defined benefit plans. If financially healthy defined benefit plans did not have to bear the costs of supporting risky plans, defined benefit plans would be more desirable to potential plan sponsors. Reporting requirements and funding standards should also be examined to determine how their costs affect the operation of defined benefit plans relative to defined contribution plans.

To forestall any further erosion in the use of defined benefit plans, policy makers should oppose new regulations that would further reduce the long-range benefits to workers and firms of negotiating these plans. Although certain provisions described above would benefit current participants, they would also further discourage the use of defined benefit plans. In effect, the welfare gains to current participants who voluntarily entered into pension contracts under the old rules will be at the expense of future workers who do not have the opportunity to negotiate these contracts.

Appendix A
Pension Coverage, CPS and SCF

Pension coverage, both defined benefit and defined contribution, in the private sector of the U.S. economy reached approximately 50 percent of the private work force in the late 1970s and has fluctuated around this level during the 1980s. This evidence is in the form of pension coverage rates for various socioeconomic characteristics derived from the May 1979 and 1983 Current Population Surveys (see table A–1) and from the 1983 Survey of Consumer Finances (see table A–2).

Pension Coverage in the CPS. The two CPS supplements contain several questions about pension coverage and pension participation. Pension coverage in this analysis is conditional on both the employer providing a plan and the worker participating in it. This measure of pension coverage requires current participation by the employee and underestimates the number of workers on jobs where a pension is provided. The coverage rate for persons in the private sector working thirty-five or more hours per week declined from 55.2 percent in 1979 to 53.1 percent in 1983. Unfortunately, the surveys consulted do not include information on types of pension plans.

The likelihood that any particular worker will be covered by a pension plan on his job varies greatly with both personal and job characteristics. Persons whose jobs are covered by collective bargaining agreements are much more likely to participate in a pension plan than nonunion workers. The coverage rate for union workers in the 1983 CPS is 82 percent, down slightly from the 84 percent coverage in 1979. These rates are much higher than the 45 percent coverage rate for nonunion workers. Company size is also an important factor in determining pension coverage. Among respondents in the 1983 CPS, the coverage rate for workers in companies with fewer than 25 workers is 18 percent, compared with 80 percent for workers in companies with 1,000 or more employees.

Coverage rates increase with higher earnings. The coverage rate

117

for workers earning less than $4 per hour in the 1983 CPS is 14 percent, down considerably from the 20 percent of these low-wage workers covered by a pension in 1979. In contrast, over three-fourths of workers earning more than $15 per hour were covered by a pension. Among workers in the CPS, older employees are more likely to be covered by a pension. Only about a quarter of workers aged 16 to 24 in 1983 are covered by pensions. Pension coverage rises to 50 percent for those between 25 and 34, and is over 60 percent for workers up to age 65. Approximately 57 percent of male workers are covered by a pension in comparison with only 47 percent of female workers.

There are substantial differences in coverage rates by industry. Mining, manufacturing, and transportation have coverage rates of over 65 percent, whereas rates in retail trade, services, construction, and agriculture are 40 percent or less. Within-industry coverage rates fell between 1979 and 1983 in most sectors; however, increases occurred in transportation, finance, and the services. The overall coverage rate is also influenced by the decline in importance of the high-coverage sectors.

Coverage and Plan Type in the SCF. The Survey of Consumer Finances also is a representative national survey that includes pension coverage data. The SCF has the additional advantage of containing information on plan type. Column 2 of table A–2 reports the pension coverage rate by individual and firm characteristics. These data are for household heads. For married couples, the husband was designated as head of the household. As a result, the SCF sample has a much higher percentage of males than the CPS sample used to determine the coverage rates in table A–1. These sampling criteria yield somewhat higher coverage rates, especially for young, low-wage workers.

Columns 3 to 5 of the table A–2 report the distribution of pension participants among defined benefit plans only, defined contribution plans only, and persons in both defined benefit and defined contribution plans. About 72 percent of union participants have defined benefit coverage only whereas 7 percent have defined contribution coverage only. Although nonunion workers are much more likely to have only defined contribution coverage, the defined contribution only coverage rate for these workers is only 14 percent.

Employees of companies with less than 100 workers are much more likely to have defined contribution only coverage. This rate is 26 percent for workers in small firms compared with 9 percent in the larger firms. Only small differences are observed in defined contribution only coverage by sex and age, except for workers over the age of

118

sixty-five. There is no pattern of differential plan type coverage by earnings level.

The largest defined contribution rate by far is found in the service sector, where 27 percent of the respondents report they have defined contribution coverage only. The next highest coverage rates of defined contribution plans are found among workers in the wholesale and retail trade and finance. It is interesting to note that these are the sectors that increased in relative importance between 1979 and 1983 (table A–1).

TABLE A–1

PENSION COVERAGE BY SELECTED CHARACTERISTICS
(percent)

	Current Population Survey			
Characteristic	Distribution of Workers by Personal Characteristics, 1979	Pension Coverage, 1979	Distribution of Workers by Personal Characteristics, 1983	Pension Coverage, 1983
All workers		55.2		53.1
Union contract				
Nonunion	75.8	45.8	77.7	45.0
Union	24.2	83.7	22.3	81.8
Company size				
Less than 25	26.6	28.5	26.0	17.7
25–99	15.3	38.2	14.6	35.1
100–499	13.5	57.1	14.3	54.7
500–999	5.0	66.7	5.5	62.9
1,000 or more	39.7	80.7	39.5	79.9
Sex				
Female	35.1	47.0	38.5	47.4
Male	64.9	59.5	61.5	56.7
Age				
16–24	21.6	33.6	18.4	27.6
25–34	29.2	56.4	32.6	51.5
35–44	19.9	61.9	21.7	62.6
45–54	16.9	66.2	15.7	63.8
55–64	11.3	65.0	10.8	64.8
65 or older	1.0	27.8	0.9	29.9

(Table continues)

119

TABLE A-1 (continued)

	Current Population Survey			
Characteristic	Distribution of Workers by Personal Characteristics, 1979	Pension Coverage, 1979	Distribution of Workers by Personal Characteristics, 1983	Pension Coverage, 1983
Earnings[a]				
Less than 4.00	6.6	20.0	13.6	14.0
4.00–5.99	32.1	34.2	30.4	33.7
6.00–7.99	30.8	53.8	19.9	54.7
8.00–9.99	16.4	69.3	14.1	68.7
10.00–14.99	20.6	83.0	18.9	79.6
15.00 or more	3.5	86.3	3.2	78.1
Industry				
Agriculture	2.2	14.9	2.1	3.8
Mining	1.3	72.9	1.4	71.4
Construction	7.1	42.9	6.2	36.4
Manufacturing				
Durables	22.0	73.4	19.2	72.6
Nondurables	13.4	67.5	13.3	64.8
Transportation, communications	8.1	70.6	7.9	71.6
Trade				
Wholesale	5.8	55.1	6.3	52.9
Retail	15.0	34.6	15.0	32.8
Finance, insurance, real estate	7.6	57.9	8.1	59.9
Services	17.6	40.2	20.5	40.8

NOTE: Includes all workers working at least thirty-five hours per week in the private sector.
a. Average hourly wage rates. The 1979 figures are reported in 1983 dollars.
SOURCE: 1979 and 1983 May Supplements, Current Population Survey.

TABLE A–2
Coverage by Plan Type, 1983
(percent)

Characteristic	Distribution of Workers by Personal Characteristics	Defined Pension Benefit Coverage	Defined Benefit Coverage	Defined Contribution Coverage	Defined Benefit and Defined Contribution
		Survey of Consumer Finance			
All workers		60.6	64.3	11.1	24.7
Union contract					
Nonunion	71.0	50.6	58.6	13.8	27.6
Union	29.0	85.3	71.9	7.4	20.7
Company size					
Less than 100	27.7	30.7	50.2	25.7	24.1
100 or more	72.3	75.0	67.1	9.1	23.9
Sex					
Female	17.7	53.9	57.7	11.4	30.9
Male	82.9	62.1	65.5	11.0	23.5
Age					
16–24	7.6	31.9	67.8	11.9	20.3
25–34	29.2	56.7	65.7	8.6	25.7
35–44	26.2	66.0	63.3	9.8	27.0
45–54	19.9	69.8	66.3	11.4	22.3
55–64	14.9	65.6	58.8	17.3	23.9
65 or older	1.9	49.1	59.7	23.0	17.4
Earnings[a]					
Less than 4.00	8.8	12.6	39.5	18.4	42.1
4.00–5.99	15.4	34.6	71.3	10.4	18.2
6.00–7.99	15.9	49.9	50.8	16.8	32.4
8.00–9.99	15.6	74.1	67.5	10.4	22.1
10.00–14.99	28.2	74.5	67.4	8.4	24.2
15.00 or more	16.0	83.8	63.1	12.6	24.3
Industry					
Agriculture	3.7	3.8	100.0	0	0
Mining	1.5	66.1	81.3	5.4	13.2
Construction	8.0	47.1	67.0	9.8	23.2
Manufacturing					
Durables	13.7	75.3	71.2	8.3	20.5
Nondurables	11.4	71.7	67.5	8.1	24.4

(Table continues)

121

TABLE A-2 (continued)

Characteristic	Distribution of Workers by Personal Characteristics	*Survey of Consumer Finance*			Defined Benefit and Defined Contribution
		Defined Pension Benefit Coverage	Defined Benefit Coverage	Defined Contribution Coverage	
Transportation, communications	9.3	72.3	72.0	6.4	21.6
Trade					
Wholesale	3.7	55.8	60.0	13.3	26.8
Retail	10.9	41.2	59.0	11.5	29.5
Finance, real estate	5.2	62.1	60.1	10.9	29.0
Services	24.6	50.4	39.8	27.3	32.9

NOTE: Includes all employees working at least thirty-five hours per week in the private sector.
a. Average hourly wage rates in 1983 dollars.
SOURCE: 1983 Survey of Consumer Finances.

Appendix B

Changes in Defined Benefit Coverage

TABLE B-1

CHANGES IN DEFINED BENEFIT COVERAGE, BY INDUSTRY, 1977–1985

Industry	Change
All Industries	−13.4[a]
Agriculture, Forestry, and Fisheries	−17.2[a]
Agricultural production[b]	−16.3[c]
Agricultural services, forestry, fishing	−15.1[d]
Mining	−18.8[a]
Metal, coal, and nonmetallic mining[b]	−13.9[a]
Crude petroleum and natural gas extraction	−19.9[a]
Construction	−17.1[a]
Manufacturing	−10.6[a]
Food and kindred products	
Meat products	−8.6
Dairy products[b]	−11.6[a]
Canned and preserved fruits and vegetables[b]	−2.6
Bakery products	−4.2
Beverage industries[b]	−6.2
Miscellaneous food preparations[b]	−11.8[a]
Textile mill products	
Knitting mills[b]	−14.4
Miscellaneous textile mill products[b]	−8.6[d]
Apparel and other finished textile products	
Apparel and accessories, except knit[b]	−5.2
Miscellaneous fabricated textile products[b]	−1.7
Paper and allied products	
Pulp, paper, and paperboard mills	−2.7
Miscellaneous paper and pulp products[b]	−12.8[a]
Printing, publishing, and allied industries	

(Table continues)

123

TABLE B-1 (continued)

Industry	Change
Newspaper publishing and printing	−5.8[d]
Other printing and publishing industries	−8.6[c]
Chemicals and allied products	
Drugs	−2.4
Soaps and cosmetics	−4.8
Plastics, synthetics, paints, and chemicals[b]	−8.7[a]
Petroleum and coal products[b]	1.4
Rubber and miscellaneous plastics products	
Rubber products, plastic footwear, hose, belting[b]	−1.5
Miscellaneous plastics products	−11.4[c]
Leather and leather products	
Footwear, except rubber and plastic[b]	−1.7
Other leather and leather products[b]	−12.3
Lumber and wood products	
Logging, sawmills, planing mills, mill work	−15.9[a]
Miscellaneous wood products	−1.7
Furniture and fixtures	−12.1[c]
Stone, clay, glass, and concrete products	
Cement, concrete, gypsum, and plaster products	−7.6
Stone, clay, glass, and nonmetallic mineral products	−5.7
Primary metal industries	
Iron and steel[b]	−9.1[c]
Other primary metal industries[b]	−9.5[d]
Machinery, except electrical	
Engines, turbines, and farm machinery[b]	−8.5
Construction and material-handling machines[b]	−11.3[d]
Metalworking machinery[b]	−8.0
Office, electronic computing, and other equipment	−10.6[a]
Electrical machinery, equipment, and supplies	
Household appliances[b]	−4.0
Radio, TV, and communication equipment	−24.4[a]
Electrical machinery, equipment, and supplies	−18.9[a]
Transportation equipment	
Motor vehicles and motor vehicle equipment	−11.2[c]
Aircraft and parts	−7.8
Boat building and repairing	−20.0[c]
Miscellaneous transportation equipment	3.5
Other fabricated metal products	
Cutlery, handtools, and structural metal products[b]	−10.0[a]
Metal forgings and stampings[b]	−9.9[d]
Miscellaneous fabricated metal products[b]	−9.4[a]
Professional and photographic equipment and watches	

TABLE B-1 (continued)

Industry	Change
Scientific and controlling instruments	−10.3
Optical and health supplies, photographic equipment, watches	1.0
Miscellaneous manufacturing industries[b]	−12.9[a]
Transportation, Communications, and Other Public Utilities	−13.7[a]
Transportation	
Railroads[b]	−12.3[d]
Local and interurban passenger transit[b]	−24.0[a]
Trucking and warehousing	−14.8[a]
Air transportation	−15.0[d]
Other transportation and services	−15.4[a]
Communications	
Radio and television broadcasting	−13.4[d]
Telephone, telegraph, and communication services	−21.2[a]
Utilities and sanitary services	
Electric light and power	−0.8
Gas and steam supply systems	−2.9
Water supply, sanitary services, and other combinations	−3.0
Wholesale Trade	−8.7[a]
Durable goods	
Motor vehicles and equipment[b]	−16.1[d]
Electrical goods	−3.1
Hardware, plumbing, and heating supplies	−9.9
Machinery, equipment, and supplies	−5.7
Other wholesale durable goods	−5.9
Nondurable goods	
Paper and paper products	−10.0
Groceries, farm, and related products	−6.8
Other wholesale durable goods[b]	−11.0[c]
Retail Trade	−11.4[a]
Building materials, hardware, garden supply, mobile homes[b]	−26.7[a]
General merchandise	1.4
Food stores	−9.0[c]
Motor and miscellaneous vehicle dealers	−8.2
Auto and home supply, gasoline service stations	−23.0[c]
Apparel and accessory stores	−12.7[c]
Home furnishings, household appliances, TV, and radio	−20.6[c]
Eating and drinking places	−12.9[c]
Miscellaneous retail stores[b]	−6.2
Finance, Insurance, and Real Estate	−10.9[a]

(Table continues)

TABLE B-1 (continued)

Industry	Change
Banking	−9.0[a]
Credit agencies and commodity services	−7.9[a]
Insurance	−5.1[c]
Real estate and real estate–insurance–law offices	−24.1[a]
Services	−19.6[a]
Business and repair services	
Advertising, business management, consulting services	−12.4[c]
Other business services	−18.9[a]
Repair and automotive services	−12.1
Hotels and lodging	−20.1[c]
Personal services	−14.4[d]
Entertainment and recreation services	−26.5[a]
Medical and health services	
Professional medical services	−6.4
Hospitals	−9.2[a]
Nursing and personal care facilities	−17.5[c]
Miscellaneous health services	−19.6[a]
Other services	
Legal services	−31.0[a]
Engineering, architectural, surveying, scientific services	−14.5[a]
Education and other miscellaneous services	−19.8[a]

a. Estimated coefficients are significantly different from zero at .01 confidence level.
b. Industries in which total employment declined between 1977 and 1985.
c. Estimated coefficients are significantly different from zero at .05 confidence level.
d. Estimated coefficients are significantly different from zero at .10 confidence level.

Notes

CHAPTER 1: PENSIONS AND REGULATION

1. Individual retirement plans or severance pay systems are often negotiated for top management. Current tax policies do not give these plans preferential tax treatment. Therefore, these deferred compensation systems typically are not funded.

2. For an assessment of pre-ERISA pensions, see Richard Ippolito, "A Study of the Regulatory Impact of ERISA," *Journal of Law and Economics*, vol. 41 (April 1988), pp. 85–126.

CHAPTER 2: DEFINED CONTRIBUTION PENSION PLANS

1. U.S. Bureau of Labor Statistics (BLS), *Employee Benefits in Medium and Large Firms, 1986*, Bulletin no. 2281, 1987, p. 77.

2. Primary pension plans refer to the main retirement plans covering workers. A supplemental plan is an additional plan provided by the firm. Many companies have traditionally used a defined benefit plan as the primary pension plan and have added supplementary defined contribution plans to increase retirement benefits in lieu of expanding the existing defined benefit plan. This analysis of the 5500 data does not include defined contribution plans that are used to supplement defined benefit plans or other defined contribution plans.

3. Dan McGill, *Fundamentals of Private Pensions* (Homewood, Ill.: Richard Irwin, 1984).

4. Small firms and self-employed workers often use Keogh plans or simplified employee pensions.

5. BLS, *Employee Benefits*, pp. 77–78.

CHAPTER 3: DEFINED BENEFIT PENSION PLANS

1. U.S. Bureau of Labor Statistics (BLS), *Employee Benefits in Medium and Large Firms, 1986*, Bulletin no. 2281, 1987, pp. 53, 60.

2. According to information on the 5500 forms for primary plans, over 70 percent of defined benefit plan participants in primary plans with 100 participants or more are covered by a formula that determines benefits as a percentage of salary average (either final or career) times years of service.

3. Steven Allen and Robert Clark, "Unions, Pension Wealth, and Age-

127

Compensation Profiles," *Industrial and Labor Relations Review* (July 1986), pp. 502–17.

4. President's Commission on Pension Policy, *Interim Report*, November 1980; Alicia Munnell, *The Economics of Private Pensions* (Washington, D.C.: Brookings Institution, 1980), p. 14.

5. BLS, *Employee Benefits*, p. 54.

6. Urban Institute, "Financial Retirement Incentives in Private Pensions," unpublished paper submitted to the U.S. Department of Labor, 1982.

7. Francis King, "Indexing Retirement Benefits," *Gerontologist* (December 1982), pp. 488–92.

8. Steven Allen, Robert Clark, and Daniel Sumner, "Post-Retirement Adjustments of Pension Benefits," *Journal of Human Resources* (Winter 1986), pp. 118–37.

9. Allen and Clark, "Unions, Pension Wealth and Age-Compensation Profiles."

10. Allen, Clark, and Sumner, "Post-Retirement Adjustments of Pension Benefits."

11. A detailed explanation of how these formulas are derived is presented in Steven Allen, Robert Clark, and Ann McDermed, "Job Mobility, Older Workers and the Role of Pensions," unpublished final report to Department of Labor, 1986. This study also includes numerical analyses of each of these plans.

12. Richard Ippolito, *Pensions, Economics, and Public Policy* (Homewood, Ill.: Dow Jones Irwin, 1986).

13. Eugene Brigham, *Financial Management: Theory and Practice* (New York: Dryden Press, 1985).

CHAPTER 4: PENSIONS AND EMPLOYMENT CONTRACTS

1. Gary Becker, *Human Capital* (New York: Columbia University Press, 1975); Jacob Mincer, *Schooling, Experience, and Earnings* (New York: Columbia University Press, 1974).

2. Robert Hall, "Importance of Lifetime Jobs in the U.S. Economy," *American Economic Review* (September 1982), pp. 716–24.

3. See, for example, Edward Lazear, "Why Is There Mandatory Retirement?" *Journal of Political Economy* (December 1979), pp. 1261–84.

4. Pension wealth from one year to the next also increases owing to a survival factor. Since a worker aged forty is one year closer to retirement than when he was age thirty-nine, the present value of a retirement benefit is greater for the forty-year-old than is the present value of the same monthly benefit to a thirty-nine-year-old.

5. This model is developed in Jeremy Bulow, "What Are Corporate Pension Liabilities?" *Quarterly Journal of Economics* (August 1982), pp. 435–52.

6. For a detailed development of this model, see Richard Ippolito, "The Labor Contract and True Economic Pension Liabilities," *American Economic Review* (December 1985), pp. 281–99.

7. The justification of this model and the related mathematics can be

found in Bulow, "What Are Corporate Pension Liabilities?"; Robert Clark and Ann McDermed, "Earnings and Pension Compensation: The Effect of Eligiblity," *Quarterly Journal of Economics* (May 1986), pp. 341–61; Lawrence Kotlikoff and David Wise, "Labor Compensation and the Structure of Private Pensions," in David Wise, ed., *Pensions, Labor and Individual Choice* (Chicago: University of Chicago Press, 1975), pp. 55–88.

8. Pension wealth is

$$V(A) = B(A) \times H(A),$$

where $B(A)$ is the benefit available at retirement (R) based on current earnings and $H(A)$ is the expected value of a life annuity of \$1 per year beginning at age R discounted to age A. Before the retirement age, pension compensation is given by

$$dV/dy = dB/dy \times H(A).$$

For work after the normal retirement age, pension compensation is

$$dV/dy = dB/dy \times H(A) - B(A).$$

9. This is demonstrated in Kotlikoff and Wise, "Labor Compensation and the Structure of Private Pensions."

10. For empirical evidence on the posteligibility effect of pensions on earnings, see Clark and McDermed, "Earnings and Pension Compensation."

11. James Pesando, "The Usefulness of the Wind-up Measure of Pension Liabilities," *Journal of Finance* (August 1985), pp. 927–40; Richard Ippolito, *Pensions, Economics and Public Policy* (Homewood, Ill.: Dow-Jones Irwin, 1986).

12. Steven Allen, Robert Clark, and Ann McDermed, "Job Mobility, Older Workers, and the Role of Pensions," unpublished final report to U.S. Department of Labor, October 1986.

13. For a more detailed discussion of the algorithm used in these analyses, see Clark and McDermed, "Earnings and Pension Compensation."

14. U.S. Department of Health and Human Services, *Vital Statistics of the United States: 1982*, vol. 2, 1986.

15. Ippolito, *Pensions, Economics and Public Policy*; Robert Clark and Ann McDermed, "Do Employment Contracts Alter Earnings Profiles?" North Carolina State University Working Paper no. 121 (Raleigh: April 1988); Ippolito, "The Labor Contract."

16. Bradley Schiller and Randall Weiss, "The Impact of Private Pensions on Firm Attachment," *Review of Economics and Statistics* (August 1979), pp. 369–80.

17. Olivia Mitchell, "Fringe Benefits and Labor Mobility," *Journal of Human Resources* (Spring 1982), pp. 286–98.

18. Olivia Mitchell, "Fringe Benefits and the Cost of Changing Jobs," *Industrial and Labor Relations Review* (October 1983), pp. 70–78.

19. Richard Freeman, "The Exit-Voice Tradeoff in the Labor Market: Unionism, Job Tenure, Quits and Separations," *Quarterly Journal of Economics* (1980), pp. 643–73; Duane Leigh, "Unions and Nonwage Racial Discrimination," *Industrial and Labor Relations Review* (1979), pp. 439–50.

20. James Rebitzer, "Establishment Size and Job Tenure," *Industrial Relations* (1986), pp. 292–302.

21. Ippolito, *Pensions, Economics, and Public Policy*.

22. Richard Ippolito, "Why Federal Workers Don't Quit," *Journal of Human Resources* (Spring 1987), pp. 281–99.

23. Steven Allen, Robert Clark, and Ann McDermed, "Pensions and Lifetime Jobs," unpublished North Carolina State University Working Paper, January 1988.

24. Steven Allen, Robert Clark, and Ann McDermed, "Why Do Pensions Reduce Mobility," in Barbara Dennis, ed., *Industrial Relations Research Association Fortieth Annual Proceedings* (Madison, Wis.: Industrial Relations Research Association, 1988), pp. 204–12.

25. An early example of such retirement studies is Joseph Quinn, "Microeconomic Determinants of Early Retirement," *Journal of Human Resources* (1977), pp. 329–46.

26. For a discussion of this technique, see Gary Fields and Olivia Mitchell, *Retirement, Pensions and Social Security* (Cambridge, Mass.: MIT Press, 1984).

CHAPTER 5: PENSION WEALTH AND JOB MOBILITY

1. Steven Allen, Robert Clark, and Ann McDermed, "Pensions and Lifetime Jobs: The New Industrial Feudalism Revisited," unpublished North Carolina State University Working Paper, January 1988.

2. Lawrence Atkins, *Spend It or Save It?* Washington: Employee Benefit Research Institute, 1986; and Donald Grubbs, "Study and Analysis of Portability and Reciprocity in Single-Employer Pension Funds," unpublished Final Report to U.S. Department of Labor, July 1981.

3. Steven Allen, Robert Clark, and Ann McDermed, "Job Mobility, Older Workers, and the Role of Pensions," unpublished Final Report to U.S. Department of Labor, October 1986.

4. This section is based on research reported in Robert Clark and Ann McDermed, "Pension Wealth and Job Changes: The Effects of Vesting, Portability and Lump-Sum Distributions," *Gerontologist* (August 1988), pp. 524–32.

5. These findings are based on Steven Allen, Robert Clark, and Ann McDermed, "The Pension Cost of Changing Jobs," *Research on Aging* (December 1988), pp. 459–71.

CHAPTER 6: EMPLOYER PENSIONS BEFORE 1974

1. Murray Latimer, *Industrial Pension Systems in the United States and Canada* (New York: Industrial Conference Board, 1932), provides a detailed examination of the growth and development of pensions in the United States prior to 1930. Also see National Industrial Conference Board, *Industrial Pensions in the United States* (New York: Industrial Conference Board, 1925).

2. Lists of existing pensions and a brief summary of plan characteristics of many early pensions are provided in Latimer, *Industrial Pension Systems;* Mary Conyngton, "Industrial Pensions for Old Age and Disability," *Monthly Labor Review* (1926), pp. 21–56.

3. A similar pattern of adoption of plans is reported by the National Industrial Conference Board, *Industrial Pensions in the United States.*

4. See Abraham Epstein, *Challenge of the Aged* (New York: Arno Press, 1976; reprinted from 1928 edition), p. 160. Epstein estimated that 16 percent of all employees engaged in manufacturing and mechanical industries, transportation, mining, and clerical work were covered by an old age pension from their employer.

5. Abraham Epstein estimated that only 5 to 10 percent of covered workers would qualify for benefits. See *Insecurity: A Challenge to America* (New York: Harrison Smith and Robert Haas, 1933), p. 148.

6. In his study of 370 plans, Epstein found that 72 percent of all the firms operating pensions had 1,000 or more employees. This was at a time when only 6 percent of all industrial establishments had more than 100 workers. See *Challenge of the Aged*, p. 161.

7. Latimer, *Industrial Pension Systems;* Rainard Robbins, *Impact of Taxes on Industrial Pension Plans* (New York: Industrial Relations, 1949).

8. John Corson and John McConnell, *Economic Needs of Older People* (New York: Twentieth Century Fund, 1956). The authors found that between 1929 and 1932, forty-five pension plans covering approximately 100,000 employees were discontinued in the manufacturing sector alone.

9. William Greenough and Francis King, *Pension Plans and Public Policy* (New York: Columbia University Press, 1976).

10. National Industrial Conference Board, *Industrial Pensions;* also see Jill Quandagno, *The Transformation of Old Age Security* (Chicago: University of Chicago Press, 1988); Robbins, *Impact of Taxes on Industrial Pension Plans.*

11. Latimer, *Industrial Pension Systems.*

12. Greenough and King, *Pension Plans and Public Policy.*

13. This conclusion is reached by comparing the data presented by Alicia Munnell, *The Economics of Private Pensions* (Washington, D.C.: Brookings Institution, 1982), p. 53, with the earlier data discussed above from Latimer, *Industrial Pension Systems* and Epstein, *Challenge of the Aged.*

14. For a discussion of plan provisions in use in 1960, see U.S. Bureau of Labor Statistics, *Private Pension Plan Benefits*, BLS Bulletin no. 1485, p. 196.

15. Alicia Munnell, *The Economics of Private Pensions* (Washington, D.C.: Brookings Institution, 1982), p. 53.

16. Donald Landay, "Private Pension Plan Coverage of Older Workers," *Monthly Labor Review* (August 1967), pp. 47–51.

17. Walter Kolodrubetz and Donald Landay, "Coverage and Vesting of Full-Time Employees under Private Pension Plans," *Social Security Bulletin* (November 1973), pp. 20–36.

18. For comprehensive reviews of federal tax policy affecting pensions during this period, see Robbins, *Impact of Taxes on Industrial Pension Plans;* Charles Dearing, *Industrial Pensions* (Washington, D.C.: Brookings Institution, 1954); Munnell, *Economics of Private Pensions.*

19. Robbins, *Impact of Taxes on Industrial Pension Plans.*

20. Stephen Raushenbush, *Pensions in Our Economy* (Washington, D.C.: Public Affairs Institute, 1955), p. 55.

21. A history of the union role in the increase of pension coverage is provided by Dearing, *Industrial Pensions;* Sumner Slichter, James Healy, and Robert Livernash, *The Impact of Collective Bargaining on Management* (Washington, D.C.: Brookings Institution, 1960). Three-fourths of all plans established between 1940 and 1949 and still operating in 1960 were collectively bargained; see U.S. Bureau of Labor Statistics, *Private Pension Plan Benefits,* p. 4.

22. Richard Ippolito, *Pensions, Economics and Public Policy* (Homewood, Ill.: Dow-Jones Irwin, 1986), p. 25.

23. For a trend in the combined marginal income and payroll tax rate facing workers, see Robert Barro and Chaipat Sahasakul, "Average Marginal Tax Rates from Social Security and the Individual Income Tax," *Journal of Business* (October 1986), pp. 555–67.

24. Ippolito, *Pensions, Economics and Public Policy.*

25. Charles Trowbridge, "Defined Benefit and Defined Contribution Plans," in Dallas Salisbury, ed., *Economic Survival in Retirement: Which Pension Is for You?* (Washington, D.C.: Employee Benefit Research Institute, 1982), pp. 3–34.

CHAPTER 7: COMPREHENSIVE PENSION REGULATION AND THE
CHANGING STRUCTURE OF PENSIONS, 1974 TO 1988

1. For a detailed discussion of post-ERISA legislation up to 1984, see Dan McGill, "Post ERISA Legislation," in *The Employee Retirement Income Security Act of 1974: The First Decade,* U.S. Special Committee on Aging, U.S. Senate, August 1984, pp. 45–79.

2. Richard Ippolito, "A Study of the Regulatory Impact of the Employee Retirement Income Security Act," *Journal of Law and Economics* (April 1988), pp. 85–126.

3. Ibid.

4. Further evidence on the distribution of plan types by plan size is provided by Ippolito, "A Study of the Regulatory Impact of the Employee Retirement Income Security Act." Using weighted data from the 5500 forms for 1982, he finds a strong interrelationship among union status, firm size, and participation in a defined contribution plan. Among pension-covered workers, only 13 percent of participants in collectively bargained plans with less than 100 participants are in defined contribution plans, and less than 1 percent of participants in union plans with more than 10,000 participants are in defined contribution plans. In contrast, 63 percent of nonunion participants in small plans are in defined contribution plans.

CHAPTER 8: EXPLAINING THE TREND TOWARD DEFINED CONTRIBUTION
PLANS

1. The link between the theoretical models of pension and plan type coverage and empirical specifications of coverage equations is described in

Robert Clark, Stephan Gohmann, and Ann McDermed, "Declining Use of Defined Benefit Plans: Is Federal Regulation the Reason?" Raleigh: North Carolina State University, Faculty working paper 119, April, 1988. Also see Stuart Dorsey, "The Economic Functions of Private Pensions," *Journal of Labor Economics* (October 1987, part 2), pp. S171–89.

2. Olivia Mitchell and Emily Andrews, "Scale Economies in Private Multi-employer Pension Systems," *Industrial and Labor Relations Review* (July 1981), pp. 522–30.

3. For the dichotomous variables like industry, union member, and education, the values represent the change in the probability of a person being covered by a pension when the value of the variable is changed from zero to one.

4. The issue of how much participants know about their pensions is examined by Olivia Mitchell, "Worker Knowledge of Pension Provisions," *Journal of Labor Economics* (January 1988), pp. 21–39.

5. A plan is determined to be a primary plan in accordance with an algorithm developed by Daniel Beller of the Department of Labor. The algorithm groups plans by the Employer Identification Number of the plan sponsor. If there is only one plan for the sponsor, the plan is deemed to be a primary plan. For sponsors with more than one plan, any defined benefit plan is considered to be the primary plan; otherwise the largest defined contribution plan is considered to be the primary plan. Thus, the algorithm biases the determination of plan type toward greater primary defined benefit coverage.

6. These estimates are in general agreement with those of Stuart Dorsey, "The Economic Functions of Private Pensions."

7. When the plan choice functions are estimated within each size group, the 1977–1945 plan choice functions are also found to be significantly different from each other.

8. To test whether the coefficients in the two equations are significantly different from each other, the equations must have the same variables. Therefore, the specification is modified to meet this requirement by dropping all of the effective date variables. These variables are deleted from the specification for this comparison because over time the weights of these variables will change because of new plan starts and terminations.

9. Alan Gustman and Thomas Steinmeier, "The Stampede toward Defined Contribution Pension Plans: Fact or Fiction?" (Unpublished working paper, August 1989) have also examined the trend toward greater reliance on defined contribution plans. Their analysis focuses on all primary plans weighted by the number of participants. They conclude that half the decline in the incidence of defined benefit plans is attributable to the plan choice process and half to structural changes. In comparison, our examination of the plan choice process of firms indicates a somewhat smaller effect attributable to structural changes in the economy. This difference appears to be due to (1) their analysis of individual plans versus our examination of the firm's choice to offer at least one defined benefit plan and (2) their use of a union variable that is available only for 1977.

10. Jack W. Wilson, Richard Sylla, and Charles P. Jones, "Financial Market Panics and Volatility in the Long Run," in Eugene White, ed., *The Stock Market Crash in Historical Perspective* (New York: Dow Jones-Irwin, forthcoming).

11. Congressional Research Service of the Library of Congress, "Private Pension Plans: Which Way Are They Headed?" prepared for the Select Committee on Aging, House of Representatives, Ninety-ninth Congress, Committee Publication no. 99-507, 1985.

12. U.S. Department of Labor, *Handbook of Labor Statistics* (Washington, D.C.: United States Government Printing Office, 1980).

13. Council of Economic Advisers, *Economic Report of the President*, January 1989.

CHAPTER 9: PROSPECTS FOR THE FUTURE

1. This raises an interesting question of how pension coverage will respond to the tax changes of the 1980s. Prior to these reductions in the tax rates and reductions in the number of tax brackets, most persons could expect their tax rates to be lower in retirement than during their working years. Now, fewer people will expect to be in lower tax brackets in retirement, and there is considerable uncertainty over whether future tax rates will be raised. In this environment, the expected gain from tax-deferred income has fallen. It remains to be seen whether workers will respond by selecting less generous and fewer pensions.

2. Employee Benefit Research Institute, "Pension Portability and Benefit Adequacy," *EBRI Issue Brief* (July 1986); Alicia Munnell, *The Economics of Private Pensions* (Washington: Brookings Institution, 1982).

3. Pat Choate and J. K. Linger, *The High Flex Society* (New York: A. A. Knopf, 1986).

4. Employee Benefit Research Institute, "Pension Portability and What It Can Do for Retirement Income," *EBRI Issue Brief* (April 1987).

5. Bureau of Labor Statistics, *BLS Reports on Employee Benefits in Medium and Large Firms in 1988*, April 4, 1989.

Bibliography

Allen, Everett, Joseph Melone, and Jerry Rosenbloom. *Pension Planning*. Homewood, Ill.: Richard Irwin, 1981.

Allen, Steven, and Robert Clark. "Unions, Pension Wealth and Age-Compensation Profiles." *Industrial and Labor Relations Review* 39:502–17.

Allen, Steven, Robert Clark, and Ann McDermed. "Job Mobility, Older Workers, and the Role of Pensions." Final Report for Department of Labor Contract no. J-9-MS-0049, October 1986.

———. "Pension Cost of Changing Jobs." *Research on Aging* 10:459–71.

———. "Pensions and Lifetime Jobs: The New Industrial Feudalism Revisited." North Carolina State University, Department of Economics and Business, Faculty Working Paper no. 116. Raleigh, January 1988.

———. "Why Do Pensions Reduce Mobility?" In *Industrial Relations Research Association Fortieth Annual Proceedings*, edited by Barbara Dennis. Madison, Wis.: Industrial Relations Research Association, 1988, pp. 204–12.

Allen, Steven, Robert Clark, and Daniel Sumner. "Post-Retirement Adjustments of Pension Benefits." *Journal of Human Resources* 21:118–37.

Atkins, Laurence. *Spend It or Save It?* Washington: Employee Benefit Research Institute, 1986.

Becker, G. S. *Human Capital*, 2d ed. New York: Columbia University Press, 1975.

Brigham, Eugene. *Financial Management: Theory and Practice*. New York: Dryden Press, 1985.

Bulow, Jeremy. "What Are Corporate Pension Liabilities?" *Quarterly Journal of Economics* 97:435–52.

Choate, Pat, and J. K. Linger. *The High-Flex Society*. New York: A. A. Knopf, 1986.

Clark, Robert, and Ann McDermed. "Do Employment Contracts Alter Earnings Profiles?" North Carolina State University, Department of Economics and Business, Faculty Working Paper no. 121. Raleigh, April 1988.

————. "Earnings and Pension Compensation: The Effect of Eligibility." *Quarterly Journal of Economics* 99:341–61.

Clark, Robert, Stephan Gohmann, and Ann McDermed. "Declining Use of Defined Benefit Pensions: Is Federal Regulation the Reason?" North Carolina State University, Department of Economics and Business, Faculty Working Paper no. 119. Raleigh, April 1988.

Corson, John, and John McConnell. *Economic Needs of Older People.* New York: Twentieth Century Fund, 1956.

Dearing, Charles. *Industrial Pensions.* Washington, D.C.: Brookings Institution, 1954.

Employee Benefit Research Institute. "Pension Portability and What It Can Do for Retirement Income." *EBRI Issue Brief* 65 (April 1987).

————. "Pension Portability and Benefit Adequacy." *EBRI Issue Brief* 56 (July 1986).

Epstein, Abraham. *The Challenge of the Aged.* New York: Arno Press, 1976. (Reprint, based on first edition published by Vanguard Press, 1928.)

————. *Insecurity: A Challenge to America.* New York: Harrison Smith and Robert Haas, 1933.

Fields, Gary, and Olivia Mitchell. *Retirement, Pensions, and Social Security.* Cambridge, Mass.: MIT Press, 1984.

Greenough, William, and Francis King. *Pension Plans and Public Policy.* New York: Columbia University Press, 1976.

Grubbs, Donald. "Study and Analysis of Portability and Reciprocity in Single-Employer Pension Funds." Final Report for U.S. Department of Labor, July 1981.

Gustman, Alan and Thomas Steinmeier, "The Stampede toward Defined Contribution Pension Plans: Fact or Fiction?" Unpublished working paper, August 1989.

Hall, Robert. "The Importance of Lifetime Jobs in the U.S. Economy." *American Economic Review* 72:716–24.

Ippolito, Richard. *Pensions, Economics and Public Policy.* Homewood, Ill.: Dow Jones-Irwin, 1986.

————. "A Study of the Regulatory Impact of the Employee Retirement Income Security Act." *Journal of Law and Economics* 31:85–126.

————. "The Labor Contract and True Economic Pension Liabilities." *American Economic Review* 75:1031–43.

————. "Why Federal Workers Don't Quit." *Journal of Human Resources* 22:281–99.

King, Francis. "Indexing Retirement Benefits." *Gerontologist* 22:488–92.

Kolodrubetz, Walter, and Donald Landay. "Coverage and Vesting of Full-Time Employees under Private Retirement Plans." *Social Security Bulletin*, November 1973, pp. 20–36.

Kotlikoff, Lawrence, and David Wise. "Labor Compensation and the Structure of Private Pensions." In *Pensions, Labor, and Individual Choice*, edited by David Wise. Chicago: University of Chicago Press, 1975.

Landay, Donald. "Private Pension Plan Coverage of Older Workers." *Monthly Labor Review*, August 1967, pp. 47–51.

Latimer, Murray. *Industrial Pension Systems in the United States and Canada*. New York: Industrial Relations Counselors, 1932.

Lazear, Edward. "Why Is There Mandatory Retirement?" *Journal of Political Economy* 87:1261–84.

———. "Agency, Earnings Profiles, Productivity and Hours Restrictions." *American Economic Review* 71:606–20.

McGill, Dan. *Fundamentals of Private Pensions*. Homewood, Ill.: Richard Irwin, 1984.

———. "Post-ERISA Legislation." In *The Employee Retirement Income Security Act of 1974: The First Decade*. Report prepared for the U.S. Senate Special Committee on Aging. Washington, D.C.: Government Printing Office, August 1984, pp. 45–79.

Mincer, Jacob. *Schooling, Experiences, and Earnings*. New York: Columbia University Press, 1974.

Mitchell, Olivia. "Fringe Benefits and Labor Mobility." *Journal of Human Resources* 17:286–98.

Munnell, Alicia. *Pensions for Public Employees*. Washington, D.C.: National Planning Association, 1979.

———. *The Economics of Private Pensions*. Washington, D.C.: Brookings Institution, 1982.

National Industrial Conference Board. *Industrial Pensions in the United States*. New York, 1925.

Pesando, James. "The Usefulness of the Wind-up Measure of Pension Liabilities." *Journal of Finance* 40:927–40.

President's Commission on Pension Policy. *An Interim Report*. Washington, D.C.: Government Printing Office, November 1980.

Quandagno, Jill. *The Transformation of Old Age Security*. Chicago: University of Chicago Press, 1988.

Quinn, Joseph. "Microeconomic Determinants of Early Retirement." *Journal of Human Resources* 12:329–46.

Raushenbush, Stephen. *Pensions in Our Economy*. Washington, D.C.: Public Affairs Institute, 1955.

Robbins, Rainard. *Impact of Taxes on Industrial Pension Plans*. New York: Industrial Relations Counselors, 1949.

Schiller, Bradley, and Randall Weiss. "The Impact of Private Pensions on Firm Attachment." *Review of Economics and Statistics* 61:369–80.

Slichter, Summer, James Healy, and Robert Livernash. *The Impact of*

Collective Bargaining on Management. Washington, D.C.: Brookings Institution, 1960.

Trowbridge, Charles. "Defined Benefit and Defined Contribution Plans." In *Economic Survival in Retirement: Which Pension Is for You?*, edited by Dallas Salisbury. Washington, D.C.: Employee Benefit Research Institute, 1982.

U.S. Bureau of Labor Statistics. *Employee Benefits in Medium and Large Firms, 1986.* Washington, D.C.: Government Printing Office, 1987.

————. *Labor Mobility and Private Pension Plans.* BLS Bulletin no. 1407. Washington, D.C.: Government Printing Office, 1964.

————. *Private Pension Plan Benefits.* BLS Bulletin no. 1485. Washington, D.C.: Government Printing Office, 1966.

U.S. Department of Health and Human Services. *Vital Statistics of the United States: 1982,* vol. 2. Hyattsville, Md.: Government Printing Office, 1986.

Urban Institute. "Financial Retirement Incentives in Private Pensions." Report submitted to the U.S. Department of Labor. Washington, D.C., 1982.

Wilson, Jack, Richard Sylla, and Charles Jones. "Financial Market Panics and Volatility in the Long Run." In *The Stock Market Crash in Historical Perspective,* edited by Eugene White. New York: Dow-Jones Irwin, forthcoming).

Index

Administrative workers, 11, 27–30
Age Discrimination in Employment Act
of 1986 (ADEA), 78
Age requirements, 74, 78
Agriculture sector
pension coverage, 94, 96
plan choice, 83, 84, 87, 89, 96, 98,
100, 101
American Express Company, 64
Assets reversion, 113–14

Baltimore & Ohio Railroad Company, 64
Banking and finance
average plan provisions, 30
pension coverage, 62, 64, 96
pension penalty, 60, 61
plan choice, 83, 84, 86, 87, 89, 96, 98,
100, 101
Bankruptcy, 32
Benefit formulas, 19–20, 27–30
Benefit limits, 75
Breaks in service, 74, 78
Budget deficit effects, 7

Career-earnings formula, 20, 32
Cash-outs. *See* Lump-sum distributions
Choice of pension plan. *See* Pension plan
choice
Civil service, 47
Clay, Howard, 113
Clerical workers, 27–30, 96, 98, 101, 102
Collective bargaining, 70–71. *See also*
Unionism
Committee on Corporate Pension Funds
and Other Private Retirement and Wel-
fare Programs, 111
Communications industry
average plan provisions, 28–29
pension penalty, 61
plan choice, 82–84, 100
Compensation, what constitutes, 33, 39
Consolidated Omnibus Budget Recon-
ciliation Act of 1986, 78
Construction industry
average plan provisions, 28

pension coverage, 94, 96
pension penalty, 61
plan choice, 83, 84, 87, 89, 95, 96, 98,
100, 101
Contribution limits, 75–78
Current Population Survey (CPS), 91

Deficit Reduction Act of 1984, 77
Defined benefit plans
average plan provisions, 27–30
benefit formulas, 19–20
defined contribution plan compared,
2–3
features, 19
financial risks, 31
implicit employment contract, 1, 3,
4, 50, 92–93
incidence and participation, 1
inflation risks, 32, 77
insurance and funding standards,
74–75, 79
labor market risks, 31–32
lump-sum distributions, 53
maximum-benefit provisions, 22–23,
77
participation requirements, 73–74
pension wealth, 19, 50
postretirement benefit increases, 26–
27
retirement ages, 23–24
social security integration, 20–22
vesting and portability, 26, 50–53, 74
wage and service accruals past normal retirement, 24–26, 48
See also Pension plan choice
Defined contribution plans
compensation profile, 16–18
contribution limits, 75, 77
contributions past normal retirement, 48
data sources, 9–10
defined benefit plan compared, 2–3
employment behavior and, 3–4, 18,
50

139

About the Authors

ROBERT L. CLARK is a professor in the Department of Economics and Business at North Carolina State University. He is a senior fellow at the Center for the Study of Aging and Human Development at Duke University and a senior research fellow at the Center for Demographic Studies, also at Duke University. He has published widely on the economics of aging and retirement and has testified before congressional committees on those subjects. He received a B.A. from Millsaps College and an M.A. and a Ph.D. from Duke University.

ANN A. McDERMED is an assistant professor at North Carolina State University. Her current research concentrates on pensions, with a particular focus on women and job mobility. She earned a B.A. at Oregon State University and an M.A. and Ph.D. at North Carolina State University.

A NOTE ON THE BOOK

This book was edited by Venka V. Macintyre and by Dana Lane of the
publications staff of the American Enterprise Institute.
The index was prepared by Patricia Ruggiero.
The text was set in Palatino, a typeface designed by Hermann Zapf.
Coghill Book Typesetting Company, of Richmond, Virginia,
set the type, and Edwards Brothers Incorporated,
of Ann Arbor, Michigan, printed and bound the book,
using permanent, acid-free paper.

The AEI PRESS is the publisher for the American Enterprise Institute for Public
Policy Research, 1150 17th Street, N.W., Washington, D.C. 20036: *Christopher C.
DeMuth,* publisher; *Edward Styles,* director; *Dana Lane,* editor; *Ann Petty,* editor;
Andrea Posner, editor; *Teresa Fung,* editorial assistant (rights and permissions).
Books published by the AEI PRESS are distributed by arrangement with the
University Press of America, 4720 Boston Way, Lanham, Md. 20706.